LOTUS-EATING JAPAN

LOTUS-EATING JAPAN

WHO IS THIS MAN I HARDLY KNOW!

LOTTE ROY

PARTRIDGE

ISBN: Hardcover   978-1-4828-8240-7
            Softcover   978-1-4828-8239-1
            eBook   978-1-4828-8241-4

Print information available on the last page.

To order additional copies of this book, contact
Toll Free 800 101 2657 (Singapore)
Toll Free 1 800 81 7340 (Malaysia)
orders.singapore@partridgepublishing.com

www.partridgepublishing.com/singapore

Dedicated to my muse, my nemesis,
Wesley Galloway

INTRODUCTION

Japan...the *exotic* far east...

Who is this man I hardly know!

My experience is not any more unique. It is a story to be told, a warning to others, a chapter of reality rarely uncovered.

How did I end up here I find it difficult to fathom....perhaps in working back through the recent course of events may clarify the bewilderment remaining...

What sucked me in?

What pulled me tight?

What trapped my mind, believing that this was right?

An escape, my way out...how delicious it tasted,

How susceptible was my spirit to the conundrum awaiting...

When at the tipping point our reactions become irrational, our perspective warped and twisted, the filter be coated with rose-colored tint.

This world, where interplanetary connections network indiscriminately, preys on the frailty of systems. With modern tools at hand, they stealthily encroach, the system we entrust only loosely securing the surface.

What we will discover is yet to be revealed, by not pursuing this notion, have we failed to really live?

MYOPIC VISION

No, that is not how I see it!

If perception be everything, then the singular impression conjured merely reflects a shard of what lies before us…

Great scholars the past over have wrestled with such theories of cognition, for they are a plenty, analyzing man's response to the world surrounding; sensations goading our vision, toying with our mind, the very experience affecting how *I* see things.

Among them, one need only look to the great sages of old, to the likes of Plato and his views; of mind-independence, tapping into a well of knowledge veridically attested, at each and every nexus, of what comes between us. Like that of a silhouette; shadowy contrasts delineating, pressing upon us a need to *fill it in*, a sliver of reality awakened.

There was of course Kant, where introspection would play a pivotal role in tackling the world around us. Of assumptions *a priori* lent to conceive ideas of substance. Perception was deduced theoretically, giving form to meaning.

What's more, and commonly quoted, the theories of Descartes, this delicate swing of balance between knowledge as recognized experience, with that of conviction, of defining reasoning. Subjecting the mechanics of vision be charged with interpretation, of delving into our belief system and questioning our certainty…the very essence of our being as quoted time and time again is, to think…therefore I am.

Are we not clouded by our own self-interest, veiled by our misunderstandings, corrupted by the misinformation feeding the 'motherboard'…our brain? Codes are registered, patterns of behavior integrated, streams of input expressed…we are, if nearly then surely, programmed to think, act and react no differently to the robotic functions of a mechanical doll, an automaton if you will…

Naturally the variables are wide reaching, the depth and breadth offering a degree of curiosity, of intrigue, yet essentially the premise by which we operate is set by some kind of 'ministry of the higher realm'....dictating and presupposing our interaction, with, may I interject, a predilection of the male persuasion....

Look no further than the shores of this nation, of male dominance supreme, constraining all manner of behavior. Structure, as set by this regulatory body of men, of communication, of character, of code, is principled on what is *proper* in social protocol. The language system of yore, standing the test of time, a system heavily loaded with the machinations of *man*-kind.

As acceptable formalities, heads of ministries are called upon, (nary a trace of the *other's influence*; shall we dare to mention the female of gender?) for they are the officials of mass education pledging wholeheartedly allegiance to the system.

The current syntax of exchange, with its foundations rooted since post World War Two; a time when the ways of the world had crumbled and suffered at the hands of such *male*-volence.

With the revision to the Constitution of the country contemplated, so too, were the choice of characters as required for any reading of official government documents. The list, for it is extensive, a number hovering just over 2,000, even now serves to ingrain the necessary measures of functionality in a nation only just recently heaving a sigh of relief from the explosion of productivity.

The standardized characters as set for the curriculum, are to be input, memorized and parroted on demand, as fulfilling exigencies of this land. And since that time, not much has been of revision, the societal acceptance by both sides of the system.

As a segue, let's reflect on humanity's revolution, on the *milestones* of our evolution.

In the animal kingdom, for which we share remarkable similarities no different from an ape or chimpanzee, the physically more competent served to protect and control, as was attested in battles many years ago. The weaker were no contest for them, and so social mores were shaped by such primeval urges; I am stronger, and therefore more powerful, so I decide what *you* do.

As in many a society long in the tooth, the leadership of chiefs, of captains, of men, would insist on preventing *the gentle folk* any exploration beyond the parameters that shelter, of *their* bed. With humiliating admittance, this necessity to insist on such proprietary domicile would be carried out in some communities right up to this the 21st century.

The alpha-male would go about his way, no different as today, protecting and defending, ensuring the security of his clan. The dichotomy existing determined the boundaries of function; the gentle folk were to remain indoors, passively awaiting their hunters, their warriors to return.

If it weren't for them, in the collective sense, no woolly mammoth nor a saber-toothed tiger would be valiantly met, strategic co-operation in the hunting was planned, in the slaughtering and quartering among the community of men. Methods developed, techniques mastered, the courage of the menfolk measured in their prize.

Whiling away the time, the women folk would sit, raising their offspring, or perhaps some cleaning of the dwelling, wondering what offerings would be of the taking. Stemming from this time, of cave-man existence, we learnt to coin the phrase *bringing home the bacon*...literally!

Of this period long ago, the organization of the home and hearth, centered around the management by the womenfolk. Socially speaking structure took form, a network of exchanges, of enterprise, a support system of sorts. This hub of activity behind closed doors, allowed the running of things to foster, a life nurturing between mother and child to unfold. Democratic in essence, the womenfolk preserved the dignity of life, recognizing fairness at play, rights of individuals, as is our inherent nature.

Yet the men, despite their engagement on the periphery, in the hunting grounds expansive and pioneering, this quest to dominate transformed into a patriarchy centralizing; the levels of function assimilated for urbanization. Of the city jungle commanding and leading, masculinity taking over society, ordering about in a despotic fashion, of tyrannical behavior only significant in the alpha-male.

When had the mental faculties of the alpha been challenged?

Not until much later, when politics would play a pivotal role in all manner of social function. It is with respect to the Greeks that a definition of civil structure became doctrine, which stands little retracted even today. Male-centric in focus, who would have heard of any woman spouting her opinion at the *gymnasia* and *stadia,* baths and *palaestra* where only the men of letters would gather....how a few millennia have transformed this congregation! (No longer do intellects gather, well, certainly not at my gym (!), the only sounds heard are the grunts and groans of the heavily dosed protein pack.)

As attested in *his* story, the men folk have learnt to co-exist, to structure systems, to observe lineage and order, and behave accordingly.

Over time, the male of the species devised such formalities, of conduct accepting. The common good as approved by the cohorts of the establishment: *the Bastion of Standards and Compliancy* was set in stone and binding, even today, somewhat chagrinned, withstanding. We have aimlessly followed with little initiative, to dare question and confront the rigidity of their 'experiment.'

The backbone of morality as premised upon the principles our predecessors set, systemizing order, bestowing recognition, paying respect; such tenets not easily defended, yet this is what separates us from the monkeys, the chimps.

The bible as reference, but not the sole guidance admittedly, any number of historical tomes carried down from generation to generation, have spoken of securing structure, of modes of behavior, of discipline and function, and through the ages have been adopted as the yardstick of social cohesion.

What becomes of these notions of yesteryear when thrown into the 21st century? They are confounding in a *biblical way* to the revolution of science, the digital age.

Upon reflection of man's great ambitions, we have journeyed thus far, now where does this lead us? How wonderful and exciting one would hope, yet sadly our maturity has been stunted at birth. We have not advanced as a people since cave-dweller existence…in many cases fundamental urges continue to shape our predicament, for the sake of survival, of perseverance.

Not to overlook completely, the inherent sense of consciousness, empathy and morality, not to mention rationality, which supposedly define us, set us apart from other primates. Given our characteristics, we could be mistaken for believing that man is of higher being, beyond the feral beast.

Au contraire mes amis, for we need only read a newspaper, better still open any number of sites online, and realize with indignation, that the innate propensity to aspire morally and spiritually has yet to embody, if at all, such virtues of our nature.

Confounding though it seems, to acknowledge our dilemma, that we are no different from any animal coexisting on this planet, ironic really when through the ages, we have struggled with such pretense of something greater.

Letter 1:

Who is this man I hardly know!

A man living half way across the world, at sea on a shipping vessel isolated in the ocean yet possesses this presence shaking my very core. You are here with my every waking(and sleeping) thought...you are affecting my spirit in ways I have never known and allowing me to express myself in words I have never used...how can this happen?

I am consumed by your passion, and acting in ways beyond my comprehension...just yesterday I was on my commute...a very crowded train to Tokyo, I missed the handrail and fell over on the floor...my mind was lost in the thoughts of you and I didn't even realise what had happened...you are making me do things, and say things so beyond my character I am now beginning to laugh at myself...oh dear....to see you, I think I will faint!

How is this possible? You have awakened in me a sense of abandonment...to let go of fear and run with my emotions...no-one has unlocked this part of me ...and now I feel all I want to do is share these precious moments with my special someone I have only met ...

Your honesty in revealing your thoughts and feelings is noble...very few people have this courage and yet you willingly open your soul to me as if we have known each other for an eternity...I read, and re-read your every word, and am spiritually uplifted...love knows no boundaries... beyond the seas, beyond the gates, beyond the roads, beyond the barriers that defend me...

I am prepared to open fully to you...you have ignited this passion I do not recognize I had...Sharing with you my intimate thoughts...you give me the confidence to do so...without you this is not possible...

CHECKS AND BALANCES

Antigone, the Greek tragedy of Sophocles, written in 441 B.C., did reflect way back then the world at large...in assessing the stability of a state, one should measure how it regards its women.

How troubling it is for Japanese women who are bullied for having children.

While committed to their place of employment, it is not as if they are *married* to their job...hardly! As it stands they are lucky to hold a temporary posting under the guise of 'part-time employment.' Despite this impermanence, this very lack of security, the married ones are castigated for, as happenstance, falling pregnant.

At the other end of the spectrum, we see the 'powers that be' encourage this attempt to breed as the rightful duty of any married woman. Sounds contradictory, and yet media tend to, by and large, glaze over such a struggle in the community.

Either way, she cannot win ...what an imposition!... to give this much attention to women.

A woman's lot is mannishly-clad by the paradigms set by the opposite sex: male enterprise, sadly even in this the 21st century. Communication and Language, Banking and Trade, Education, Politics, Employment, Marital status and Social standing, are domains bound today by a misogynist leaning.

Women have learnt to endure at the hands of man's failings (What!... they are fallible and not God-like in their capacity...shock, horror!)Their defeats and collapse, their oversight and neglect, playing up and breaking down, their insolvency, floundering and flop...

This resilience to adversity, that very quandary only created by the masters themselves, has triggered a desperate need to bear such conditions, us womenfolk (as if we don't *bear* enough already in child birth!)

We have learnt to accept and accommodate, as is expected of us, the 'fragile' of the sexes. Yet how many among us have striven to dispute such status quo? Unfortunately a paltry sum....

The reference to women in the *his*torical context has only been measured relational to men...*their* mother, lover and wife. She was of course, the daughter, sister and niece, but scant has described the independent thinker, political actor, or public speaker, as is the story of Antigone.

An allegory for resistance nevertheless, why hasn't there been many other heroines of fortitude and strength? Incredible to realize as such a classic has withstood the test of time. What about the modern peers? I hear you cry... such role models have, with disdain, been shunned, slighted and sadly trivialized.

Since evolution, women have succumbed to the maxims as meted by men, accepting precepts, following orders with, let's be honest, little hesitation. And for a long time now, the fairer sex has been cut off from any system of order other than that of the domestic front, managing affairs (and *not* necessarily sexual either) as separate units, adhering to the household duties as weighted upon them.

What has been accepted for centuries thus far is that man dominates in all aspects of marital bonding. A notion of *equality,* dare I say, would corrupt that very sense of ownership and control, that of such a conservative outlook.

Betrothed, the wife has obsequiously sought to meet the expectations of not only her husband but invariably her in-laws...(the parameters defining the family within *their* own oblique system of what is good and proper,) as is of demand of her right up to this day.

Immobilized in marriage, since long ago, she was taken as *rightful property* under wedlock. As a side note, I am urged to comment, the curious nature of these terms property and wed-*lock;* as if doomed to be firmly kept under latch and key, a padlocked yard? Pastures lain fallow occasionally? Alas, she was never to relish in life and love, let alone her own sexuality until very recently.

Marriage then, and perhaps even now, like that of a chastity belt of the Middle Ages; by default dissuasive in control enforcing this exclusivity, not a measure of freedom in the more modern-day sense was afforded such a woman...the loaded obligation generally upheld was to perform periodically at the whim of her husband, as contractually assumed.

Even now, the *Bastion of Order and Compliancy* requires as much, yes, even today.

Women rarely had that opportunity to integrate, join forces, and luxuriate in each other's company....perhaps of the higher echelons of the privileged class this was a given, but not common practice for the ordinary 'house-bound' women...No, they were isolated, tending to the duties internal, occasionally venturing outside for some procurement, then rushing back to serve the master his supper, in the vain hope of gaining approval from the breadwinner, the ruler, the commander, the father.

Mother as home-maker: repetition, detachment, isolation.

Domestic bliss premised upon that delicate balance of approval.... of keeping the head of the house happy, and for what gain? So the gentler folk would remain secure in knowing their *lord* would protect and serve... and after each quest a bounty brought home...how we were blessed.

And what of the children?

Oftentimes, as was the life of business external, the very presence of the head would frighten the wee folk, the impression stoic and distant... a stranger of folklore, a legend spoken of... godlike in status beyond the bonding of the mother...who was he? And why did he deserve such honor? Why, of course, he was the most powerful one; the *assumed* ruler of the family...or was he?

We overlook the fact that for the majority of time, it was the mothers who had to safeguard their children, ensuring the stability of the home environment, this playing a crucial role in protecting their dependents from imminent threats. No small feat, the demands made tested the fortitude of the role laden before her, beyond expectations, beyond text book (though hardly written of and at that, rarely read until just over a century ago) merely passed down, of word of mouth, from one generation to the next (if the naive young bride were made privy to the actualities enshrouding wifedom.)

And just like some men with their cool detachment, so too were the women. Reluctant to project thoughts on matters matrimonial, socially pressured to conform; be married by the time you are in your twenties, and all else would fall 'naturally' into place.

And what of the **all else** one bemoans...how is that magically resolved? How gullible, and misdirected we have been. Not even the matriarchs would admit to the pressures of maintaining this delicate balance...juggling life's curve balls, plenty of brooding over breeding, only to be drained physically and emotionally.

And for what? I hear cried.

For security and stability…or rather, appeasing societal exigencies of servility?

Acknowledging her destiny stifling patriarchally speaking, a woman is to swiftly find a husband and settle down. Despite her personality, her wit and perspective on life, such charms only come secondary to finding the one; a partner for life.

Pity on her if she be average-looking, of not too pretty, or *even* intelligent. For she will not do well in the *jackpot* of life, of securing a honey with money as is the target.

We need not venture far for such supporting evidence…the *Hina Matsuri* or Girls' Day in Japan is a fine example. Young ladies are to be bred to be *good wives*, and *good mothers*. This celebration is to remind us of the importance of their daughters to grow healthy and strong and find *good husbands*. Not finding a partner, whose role is to shelter and protect, would bring a heavy burden on the parents, and what misfortune this would bring. Not to be left as a *Christmas cake* old and stale, oh what a shame, as it is harder to dispose of a woman past her 25th birthday. Ideally to marry soon after your 20th is considered lucky, a sigh of relief upon the immediate family.

Looking further afield records in history reveal the importance of tying the knot in your twenties.

Take for instance the French. Women of this age group, of being 25 years old, on St. Catherine's day, were to attend a formal gathering, a ball if you will, and wear atop a *chapeau* indicating her status yet a maiden. It was arranged as such to enable those approaching their prime to finally meet their suitor and settle down. Partly for the benefit of dating and for public shaming, the genuine intentions of the state were to see their young women wedded.

The Germans would, at the age of their 25th, have unmarried women be 'honored' with a wreath of boxes; "*Schachtelkranz*" a reference to old, empty containers, usually a derogative term for a difficult and unpleasant woman. Mind you it was not only the womenfolk who reminded society of failing to meet expectations. Menfolk too, were poked fun of in the public sense, by parading in costume and made to sweep the public building or ride on donkeys while facing backwards through town.

Through emancipation of the more privileged circles, social mobility soon took traction for the womenfolk. A degree of independence from their masters transpired, networks of the *kinder* sex only really came about around the Industrial Revolution; this age of *supposed* economic progress, whereby necessity to find waged work, to contribute for the greater good outside the home was more prevalent. And so, in the manner of their latter-day role models, the women would unite. Like busy ants, they too worked to set boundaries and structure civic order on their own.

As an interesting divergence allow me to revert to nature; Darwin's observations of ant nests highlights the inherent competition in social structures. The individual members, each with their designated roles; the queen, drones, and workers all collaborate in the pursuit of survival. Being paramount is group cohesion; all members fall into place, serving a greater purpose. Such observations confirm this analogy; the significance of order driving natural selection is apparent.

But where are we today? What has become of such women? The drive to stand resolute in the face of struggle, for most today in the industrialized world, seems archaic, something my grandmother spoke of bygone days!

Yielding to the powers that be, of the alpha- male domineering, women generally, have grown accustomed, and sadly accepting of man's inherent pitfalls, the problems of mismanagement, of poor leadership and, knowing no other, have fallen into the trap of mimicking what is theirs.

Even as measured progress, women are bound by the same orders defined in the male prerogative. Yes, we have achieved, climbed those rungs of *their* ladder, proven it can be done, yet where does this lead us?

To play into their palm as we have done over the ages, does nothing for carving our own interpretation. Having a voice independent of them, of setting rules, and determining paradigms as reflective of our own intentions are virtually not prevalent. The games we have become familiar, and striven to compete. Yet the subtlety of gaining position is harder to achieve. We can never fully embrace that moment of success...from the outset it is a male-dominated leaning we sadly fail to address. No matter how we try, we cannot assimilate. On principle we are not one of them.

THE LIBERATED

Of notions *noblesse*, I dare conjecture, have been washed ashore of a time misled. It is not a matter of *who* you are as individual thinkers, but how you function in the scheme of things, in rank and file only, our life superficial. Categorized, coded, in some kind of order; part of a system as classified thus, no need for thinking, just accepting your position, and press enter.

Mass media has a lot to do with it. We have succumbed to the power of mediated consumption, the penetration of mass communication, the bombardment of information permeating our daily existence, conceded to the prevailing forces, impervious to tipping this *semblance* of balance, and challenge even today what is labeled and accepted as **the 'new' normal.**

Ah the malaise of 21st century modernity; the seduction of choice...

These trappings of supposed comfort, tease us, lure us in to believing:

We have made it. We deserve it. Why not indulge!

And like sponges absorbing the latest and greatest, only to be saturated, clogging any passage of reason, asphyxiated.

As yet forming a unified voice, women have sadly failed to organize themselves, to unite as one force, to liberate from the codes and structures that bound them tight, of societal *conduit*, oh what a course.

Distracted by the shopping lists of things to have, issues pertaining to the *weaker sex* are even today sadly sidestepped; swiping pursuits in the cause of women universally, for the sake of coveting the status ascribed; meanwhile pocketing our needs and wants as consumables indeterminate.

Societal values of what defines us have become measured by our possessions, of what owns us. Pegged accordingly to income and earnings, rarely relevant are notions of women's struggle, of a global vision; the will to ignite the potential for a brighter future unilaterally speaking.

For the record may I just say, there exist a handful of phenomenal women, who have indeed with verve and conviction, rose up to confront, lead in ways incalculable given the inherent cultural dogma.

Oh dear Malala comes to mind,
Of noble pursuits, she has soared inconceivably,
In wonder of her virtuous ways, it is remarkable at such a young age.
Despite such weights of edicts yoked,
The constraints outmoded, hence amnesty invoked,
Selfless in her determination, she alone has become a beacon for many,
Persecuted though they remain,
She has shown there is hope in the struggle, in the pain.

It is rare this fortitude of such an individual. Yet on occasion, a bright spark has risen and stated without affectation, the need to challenge the system. Though the notion of female independence to some sounds dissident, snippets are prevalent in society regardless of endowment.

BUT be aware!

Those few recordings in the annals of history would compare this ascent of women as less than favorable; either the workings of the devil; witches, or the extreme as saints; all depending on interpretation. We need not wander far down that path, let it be known, just in the last few months in the running up to the U.S. election 2016, we see the candidates; a man Trump of dubious temperament chastise his opponent Clinton, (shock, horror) a woman, plainly more qualified and deserving as many would agree.

Words to the effect all damning and brutal; she is dangerous, aggressive, ludicrous, loud and vulgar.....a fine example of character assassination...far from the political agenda penned in the race for any presidency. And yet we witness today the same reaction in men to the rise of a woman....'she is not to be trusted,' menfolk be warned....'it is all in her eyes' I have heard him utter.

Frustrations of the 21st century woman do not translate well...A chapter on leading women in executive power? Allow me time to look that one up... few mentions...but only briefly...

Ah Japan!

Despite your progress to catch up economically and lead in the 21st century, how you lag behind terribly, socially speaking that is, and regrettably.

As acknowledged by the World Economic Forum, the country consistently ranks as one of the world's worst nations for gender equality at work; or equality of any nature, frankly speaking. The *Japanese way*, left unaffected since the Edo period (1603-1868), has allowed this prolonging of male privilege. For it is still said among the folk here, a married working woman is demonized as the devil wife or '*oniyome*.' Why of course she ought to be at home, breeding, and cleaning and preparing supper for his return. That defines her role in life even today....little more is expected from the *wee* wife.

The business world here fraught with sexist attitudes deeply rooted, perhaps a reference to Edo (1603-1868), or even beyond, the rungs of success favor the male worker. For the woman is a risk factor, long-term speaking.

What if she gets married? And falls pregnant?

These are notions definitely not worth considering. A bad investment indeed, she is of no intrinsic value here other than to lick stamps and seal envelopes despite the advances of technology. By sheer presence in the office, regardless of function, the *office–lady* purports that this company is *warming up* to assimilation. Alas, when scratching the surface it does appear, her role is, and remains one, to serve tea.

LOL impossible to pursue without grit determination…She must have nerves of steel, defense mechanisms immeasurable, she must make a complete sacrifice of life, of love, of partnerships and sharing, to the throes of a career, *of a professional undertaking*.…and just like childbirth, though only imagined, the painful struggle, the intensity and demand no less a burden than that of survival, her need to persist remains the duty of none less than the obedient soldier…of the corporate world…

On the global platform promotion for women has had little impact. A hierarchy of sorts, female leadership held by the mighty and the strong; despite the media denigrating the stereotypical whipping matrix corseted and sassy… For those who dare, the undertaking to strut her stuff, have an impact on the stage, to focus on challenging the established roles defining women for just over a century, this is one crusade not without its casualties sadly.

A few women of substance holding executive function, impacting on a universal scale, how many more would be exemplary. There is the head of the US central bank, Janet Yellen, Christine Lagarde in charge of the International Monetary Fund, Germany's Chancellor Angela Merkel and Theresa May as the new prime minister in the U.K., while the USA could have had its first female president, Hillary Clinton, if the votes were counted fairly that is. Despite their achievements what foreboding overshadows this scale of the glass cliff. Casting aspersions, for fear looms, of how long she will remain in office before *she* trips and falls. This insistence that one day soon, she will fail brilliantly, how the menfolk would relish this opportunity to prove disparagingly: 'I told you so.'

Letter 2:

What happiness means:

We all strive for similar goals...to be happy...but how do we define what this is? Many are of the impression that a nice car, big house with many things would satisfy their aims of being...others not so...I tend to be of the latter variety. Naturally we all like the new, and go shopping for the sake of it...we are only human...and on one level that feels good.

For true happiness to exist, a strength of character must persist, a resilience to the chaos that can upset our daily lives. Like soldiers, we must defend and protect our core values, and never let distraction eat at our essence... the nature of a survivor. To aspire to virtues of happiness without temptation is a virtue...and a tough one at that. We fall to what is easy or convenient, what fits our mood at that time...and never really be conscious of our decisions.

I sit at this precipice, ready to dive and swoop down through the valleys and mountains of life with you...a risk unbelievable. I have never been a gambler; betting to win money, but am prepared to take this step with you....and I don't really know you...how is this possible?

Instinct is driving me forward on this...and the changing circumstances edge me towards you like nothing before. To entertain the notion of one, of being whole, of being complete...gives me a sense of purpose, responsibility and honor. To sit beside you, to exchange ideas no matter how challenging, is what I truly relish...I want to enter your mind, and know what it is to be the wonderful person you are today. We won't agree on everything...this is the beauty of nature...to question and constantly stretch our curious minds of learning....you have a lot to teach me...

A few lines of a poem have given me strength throughout the years of uncertainty:

>Be yourself. Especially, do not feign affection. Neither be cynical about love; for in the face of all aridity and disenchantment it is perennial as the grass...

You are a child of the universe, no less than the trees and the stars; you a right to be here. And whether or not it is clear to you, no doubt the universe is unfolding as it should....

With all its sham, drudgery and broken dreams, it is still a beautiful world. Be careful. Strive to be happy. <

I carry this with me wherever I go...and want to share this with you... to be truly happy we must protect what it is truly beautiful....like our feelings for each other, like your daughter, like the worlds we engage in, and the stars above... I pray for this to work....

QUID PRO QUO

The footing of an individual in this social spectrum is relegated according to rank, a bit like an officer in the military sense. The higher the status, the greater the importance, hence the lower the rung, how must you earn the honor! It works in tandem, exponentially speaking, one reliant on the other, the higher the order, the greater the deference. Never is this more pronounced than here.

Only thawing from a bygone era, that of Edo period (1603–1867).

Essentially today they are of a democratic leaning. Mind you only in *geste*, you cannot simply adopt a label for convenience, and call yourselves 'democratic', a fair and balanced world, of aspirations *noblesse*. No, this is a system heavily loaded with the 'grooves of establishment,' their veins deeply throbbing still, since before the Edo period. No one can quite erase the values of yesterday, and march confidently in a fashion, to the beat of modernity. Nor can they quite fully embrace notions of a Western paradigm, their interpretation akin to the leverages of an ancient kind.

Look no further than the Imperial family; respectfully intact, despite the controversies surrounding. The household management; a panel of 16 members apparently, still dictates the approval of family members' announcements or public engagements.

A higher echelon exists controlling the royal establishment? The most revered of subjects are they themselves orchestrated in the public realm, curtailing any scrutiny, avoiding innuendo?

And thus propriety as mandate revered, trickles down to the lowest denominator socially speaking. Peering, prying, monitoring and regulating the job of their upright citizens, the purveyor of order, of cultural cohesion, of maintaining the *wa*, the homogeneity of a people.

Underpinning the society here, is this principle of *wa* or group harmony of the Japanese; the essence of being of this nationality. Avoiding contestation, very little confrontation, social cohesion is paramount to a well ordered people. There sits a place for each member of this extensive network, and everyone in their proper place be of function. Stemming from the fundamentals of Confucius thinking, harmony can only ever be achieved when honouring this hierarchy of systems. And just like a soldier all decorated, the privileges determined according to the chain of command. Observing and upholding such aspirations of uniformity can only be achieved if loyalty to the group pays heed.

Throw a *gaijin:* a foreigner, in the works, and the delicate balance of *wa* is skewered.

Just like a woven piece of silk, the tension and slack of the weave adjusted for the purpose of function and taste, society presents itself as the warp and weft of this stretched cloth before me, far-reaching and all encompassing. How is one to stitch a thread?

Recognize your place, be aware of your standing, keep the canvas tension tight enough; no gaps, nor holes perforated. Perhaps the penetration of the outsider, his presence alone stresses the threads of society, causing the knit to fray, to bleed, to unfold.

The balanced order of knots combined, creates this comforting blanket of security, and completely; the close-knitted clique...perfection of association.

As the milieu of harmony and order, those belonging to this network accept the tenets prescribed, with nary a thought to resist, neither motivation to challenge, nor need to confront the dictates codified.

As for equality, the right to be oneself, the individual; they are considered *way* too Western in motivation, somewhat Christian in ethos, and damning to social cohesion. The core values of the philosopher Confucius standing unchanged over two thousand years, still hold sway despite the advances in our world today.

By contrast we look to the West, where individual motivation drives success; in the personal, in the public, and in capital. The *Declaration of Independence*, a testimony of noble endeavours, proclaims the equality of man, endowed at birth with unalienable rights such as Life, Liberty and the pursuit of Happiness among them. Such are these principles esteemed, perhaps in some circles alas, sadly unattainable, nevertheless are ideals sought.

Upon interpretation, every man enters this world with equal footing, how you succeed depends on several factors, the greatest being: will and determination. Some make it through sheer luck...others invest their efforts to come out on top. Regardless, society tends, by and large, to give you a go, prove yourself worthy, and naturally life flows. Yes I know, let's not get too carried away, but the importance of happiness is one we are all entitled to claim. Of equality and fairness, in the broadest sense, values we aspire to despite the current malaise of the 21st century.

Inculcated are we at an early age, to consider all are essentially equal, and as such instinctively I, perhaps not all would agree, (pursue nobly, who am I kidding?) feel compelled to regard fellow mankind with respect and trust, giving the benefit of doubt as necessary. In essence to be treated fairly, friendships would generally group quite naturally, without a sense of burden, of obligation, or duty. If we 'click', we probably have an interest in pursuing the relationship further. We choose to do so out of curiosity, out of spontaneity, perhaps even receptive to the chemical charges stimulated.

There is no predict determining behaviour, how am I matched according to file and rank. And there lies the distinction; by definition the cultural impetus demarcating society, their individuals and motivation.

Acts self-deprecating?

....the belittling of the self for the sake of the other.....My humble servant, I think I am going to sneeze!

Is there a purpose to all this affectation of complaisance and humility? cries the Westerner. An ulterior motive, a hidden agenda? Or are we supposed to bow, no matter how deeply, to impress upon the sincerity of our intentions?

Maybe I am an idealist, bit wet behind the ears, but in our daily cycle, no matter how trivial, it would be considered common courtesy to give recognition in good-natured fashion, a hello to you or even a mere nod to the neighbors.

We do see such interaction at play with the older folk here; greeted in a friendly manner 'o-haiyo!': good morning. Strangely only randomly though... inconsistency exists...ah the capricious nature of such people!

One day bright and beaming; the next, blank facial expressions defensively cowering.

Reading the complexity of character was never so baffling. How are we to secure a sense of stability, of confidence in the fickle nature of such a community...never!

To communicate with such a people fearful of the other, the different, the foreign… it may be the 21ˢᵗ century with all the trappings of an advanced society but mentally or rather psychologically, attitudes have made little progress since the Edo period….ah the glories of the forefathers…so upright and strong… where did society go wrong…those pesky Westerners, with their modern ways unwelcome….why did we let them in, to corrupt our precious station?

Despite the maddening rage encroaching upon our world today, such principles of civility remain at the core of society….at least for the moment. They are the tenets by which we follow, and so we ensure to pass them down to the next generation. Sadly traces of such attitude appear to be fragments of a bygone period when the *want* and *desire* were not the driving force of man's occupation.

Inclusivity; a comforting state, exists within, and gives reason for the affinity in the closed circles, extending oneself for the greater betterment of the network. It is said the commonality of DNA make up does serve to influence reasons of altruism. All in the family we hear cried, makes more sense since identified.

Wholesome values binding a community together existed in a time when the spirit of humanity was stronger. Looking out for your family, friends, and neighbors was never so pronounced. We did what we could with the little we had, to bring comfort and perhaps joy …such humble endeavors…So what happened? Where did society shift its perspective, and draw a line defining what is correct and proper….as opposed to what seems natural or voluntary….

A favor anyone?

In some domains, here included, it will cost you!

Beyond the closed cliques existing; altruism of naturally extending goodwill, of caring and sharing… such values as catechized in our bible classes are not apparent…*unless* the dissolution of circumspect, and the roots of inclusion are well planted…for here anyway. This could take years to establish…and only then, should we be so privileged, *we* may even be considered among *them*. Far from a brotherly or sisterly sort of way, you must be deserving of the kindness at hand…random acts are rarely on the offer…selective calculation measures your worth…in effect, love is earnt.

In a society highly praised for their deferential nature, take a look closer at customer service, overwhelming in the eye of the foreigner. On the surface it would appear selfless, in a *beck and call* kind of way. Yet essentially in the exchange, two roles are being played out; the potential client with intentions to invest, and the representative for instance, reliant on this, the trade. Where does the notion of complete subjugation to my loyal client factor in this transaction? Hardly, one would say!

What is at stake begs the scenario in question: My dignity, my reputation, the hole in my hand? The interplay between the subjects is perhaps no different from that of lovers. Each having an agenda motivated by factors, of exigencies measured, needs yet requited. Certain elements attractive, drawing the individual in, touching on persuasion only subtly tinged. And like a *sonata*, the first movement shifts graciously, followed by a *serenade* more intimately, passions flare, tempers rise and subside as in the *allegro*, all in meeting our desires or compromise in the *coda*.

Often coined the Japanese way, this approach to accommodating the clients, the visitors, the guests, of offering service, in the hospitality sense, is what they call "Omotenashi." Confusion belies this definition of a notion, how do you say subjugation of the self without being servile in English? The subtlety in anticipating the exact yearnings of the patron, is the height of savvy, the epitome of civility rendered. Gauging implicitly a degree of satisfaction, without a word mentioned, impresses the client with such sensitivity to attention. How much more endearing it must be, to be offered without even asking! Mind reading? Telepathy perhaps...it never fails to bemuse me the gestures made.

Omotenashi, the simulacrum of deference, disingenuous at its core?

How are we to discern gestures in earnest? Or rather the sycophant's co-dependence?

....We, the establishment, offer a full range of services, and cater to your every need (well only to a degree.) If we glance down at the clauses, the small print, you will find an outline of the conditions stipulating the outline of our exchange; the patron behave within the boundaries expected...to challenge the establishment further would be an affront to the precious interaction. You are to recognize such codes and adhere accordingly....

Parameters of exchange are observed and controlled...the predictability of intentions; keeping abreast of the situation...ensuring no step be out of place... ah the pretense. Nothing is left to chance. Doing so, the clients' needs are premeditated, by definition assumed and weighed...and they do it with such finesse...standardized, systemized, and sorted.

Seduced immediately by this routine well rehearsed, traps the mind into thinking I am God! For the uninitiated, like honey to a bee, the magnetic impulse only enticing, exceeding our precepts beyond recognition, beyond realization.

Meted and measured, calculated and rationed with an exactitude passed on from generation to generation...oh the paradox of such a social system the Japanese way...the need for self-reliance never more pronounced than here (or perhaps in North Korea or China?)

But is that what I want begs the question. How are you to assume what I am after? Here lies the fissure cracking open the issues, of *guesstimating* what it is good and proper...may not necessarily satiate me further. We *know* what is best for you, as if reading the quack's mind in handing out potions....

The craftsman in his cunning way will wield you into believing this is indeed most befitting: You *will* appreciate my wares on offer, for they are above all else highly prized, and surely not of your far off land where *you* reside. The technique, the beauty I guarantee you know no other....and like a well-practiced snake oil doctor, the encounters only brief, to set about summoning up a proffer.

Perhaps this works well in a homogenous society where few anomalies arise...the local patron by duty or obligation, not wishing to confront nor negotiate, burying any objection to the terms, accepts the exchange, nods obediently, blindly assumes the conditions...what is best in this parody of exchange. The exhibition distracting from the essence of intentions, leads us, the patron, to believe these are experts...as for me, I have known no other.

This was never so pronounced than a visit to Kyoto recently. Though I am grateful for the experience, my observations clearly highlight the esoteric of such a notion, that of *omotenashi*.

We had been dining in a high-end *kaiseki* restaurant (a traditional multi-course Japanese dinner and is analogous to Western haute cuisine.) in the lower part of *Gion*; Kyoto's most famous geisha district, not far from the main street. The food was exceptional, as only the chefs here know how. During the course of the meal, we had developed a rapport with the head. An affable character, with a certain witty charm, he entertained us on the aspects of life in this former capital. On departing, he suggested we visit a *maiko-san*'s tea room, loosely translated as a private bar where alcohol, and *not* tea be on offer. To be granted entry in this world was by invitation only, further enshrining the *carte blanche* elevation. Incidentally a *maiko-san* is a lady in her early twenties, an apprentice preparing in all aspects of the institution of *geisha*…terribly coded… crafted…of a bygone period. For it takes years before fully accomplished, the apprenticeship of manners accustomed for being a consummate geisha

On entry to this dimly lit, unadorned establishment, no wider than an ordinary terrace in the area, and bowed down humbly low as if supplicating to favors bestowed, on a mounted platform above the entrance was the *maiko*-san herself. Be-draped in a fine silken kimono, with the nape of her neck slightly revealing, apparently considered somewhat erotic, a little daring for the visitors, set the tone as she welcomed our presence. Her elaborate costume marking her status, the details of her kimono, the *obi* or belt bound tightly around her waist, the fancy headdress mounted atop, no doubt a challenge to maintain, the several *accoutrement* reflecting the stage of her training. Painstakingly choreographed for such an occasion, we, as her guests, were to be entertained in the art of parlor games.

The language, not even that of standard Japanese, was uttered, impressing upon us the fact we had entered a special place like no other. We were mesmerized, intoxicated by the sheer otherworldliness on display.…we had stepped off this planet, had been transported back in time…and were immersed in an era reflecting 200 years ago, of Edo enshrined.

We sat in a modest setting such is the Japanese way. The service area set sunken into the *tatami*; a rush-covered straw mat forming a traditional Japanese floor covering, so in effect patrons would sit on three sides of the bar at eye level with the hostess, our *maiko*-san. Deliberately arranged in such a way this enhanced the 'personalized' treatment, and only encouraged the intimacy with the patrons. Far from any western concept of *the bar*, it was lit with an exposed fluorescent bulb, there was no menu, no advertising; simply an old ceramic urn and ladle positioned on the bench and a few washed glasses ready for service.

Side dishes were prepared in advance…only a few, and mostly reflective of the season… side dishes of salt cured cockles were served that evening…The choice of beverages as with the menu were limited in range *shouchu* local and potent; distilled liquor from either rice, barley, buckwheat or sweet potato, with no less than 45% alcohol per volume.…upon reflection more like jet fuel than a refined distilled scotch but who am I to judge, I am no *bon vivant*…regardless, this was so revered as quite a rare opportunity; to be privy to a *maiko*-san in the exclusive surroundings of the privileged…as it would appear.

The atmosphere convivial with a few more patrons; in total six sat comfortably, sharing the space, and openly conversing amongst ourselves. The *maiko*-san in her deftness quickly provided the liquid provisions, occasionally rushing into the back room, screened beyond our view. The sheer effort to remain poised with the many layers of her garment tightly bound firmly, sleeves draping at the ankle, a train restricting her stride, the need to balance her head-dress for fear of toppling; that in itself was an act of dexterity, truly admirable. When all settled, the art of repartee commenced; the skills finely tuned, with the exactitude of well- choreographed interplay. For good measure, a smattering of English was also showcased, a sense of inclusion incorporated into the exchange.

We were entertained, as defined by the *surveyors, conveyors and purveyors* of taste yesteryear. All for a pretty price I must say…a couple of hundred for each visitor…. Coiling in shock, I could become cynical, even critical of the economics at play here, but I won't.

Beguiling, mystified by the execution, we were enticed by such a display of reverence convincing us our treatment like that of royalty. But in the mind of the visitor; was that it?

Peeling away the layers, dropping all pretenses, what are we left? The core of an individual naked, lay bare. The facades, the window-dressing, the veneer all disintegrated, beyond the layers of distraction, the embellishments, the artifice, the dressage…where were we? What remains is unadulterated, the value of the self insignificant. How much weight we place on glorifying the external, only to realize the weakness a society is to the superficial. If the absolute be that all we have is you and me, isn't the very essence of humanity to identify thy true self? To deny this is to foolishly cede, relinquishing our own very nature, to the forces of expediency.

Letter 3:

Who is this man whiling away your waking hours penning your thoughts, your ideas, your love ...a prophet, a saint, an angel from above bestowing shining brilliance! A romantic poet...a rare find at that...who writes such expression in this day and age?

Just listened to the ballad of Michael Jackson...truly speechless... nothing is for real...I am floating in this universe enraptured by the warm embrace you offer across the oceans high...I stumble and fumble to make sense of my emotions...I cannot control myself...you have consumed, engulfed me, and now none of this can I explain...truly speechless...

Where have you been my soulful mate of wonder? You have chosen your timing well, and tried my patience in the waiting...yet the moment is now...I feel you, recognize you...to hold you...to be alive and relish the presence of your mind, body and spirit....

Your choice of words show a sensitivity beyond belief...I read these messages usually on my commute...and fear I will faint as my heart implodes with emotion...no-one has struck such a chord...and no-one else ever will...you have pierced my heart with a blade so sharp...I am bleeding passion inside... this raw emotion permeating my every thought process, my every action, my every day since meeting you. You have awakened in me, stirred my desire to know you, learn from you, and grow as one solid and complete...

And yet we have not met face- to face...for that day to come, I will be sick with emotion...the joy so powerful, the attraction so intoxicating...I will be a mess! The impact of your words themselves have shaken my very being beyond belief... in your physical presence I will be overcome with excitement and fear...and riding high on the wave of your love...

Are we rushing into these feelings so soon? I cannot say, but revel in the indulgence...I love you! What man is this? My fair prince...my mysterious admirer, my angel...you will always be.

I cannot hide my feelings for you, nor feign my emotions...my desire for you grows each and every time we connect...I cannot deny it... you have touched my soul so much so...I am speechless...nothing is for real...

CHURLISH GIRLISH

Of what fickle nature women are!

I should know. Being raised in an all-women environment, educated in a private-girls' college, I am no fool to the inscrutable disposition of women-folk. It is a characteristic that shields us, a barrier defending against the woes festering in society. Holding patience to the absurdities set among men...how noble an aspiration! Yet to endure requires cunning, and strength, and not of the physical sense.

Resilience means being cutthroat and ruthless...in Japan sadly no less tantamount than post World War Two. Theirs is not a society of *nodding violets (The Chrysantheum and Sword p.54)*; the mask once lifted reveals a more volitional character borne out of a need of survival.

Don't be fooled by their polite ways, the standardized choreography, they have mastered and conditioned, how they play. Receptive to their gestures of hospitality, the visitor responds, and naturally so, to the appearance of generosity, this affording us a sense of comfort welcoming.

Dispelling such myths we discover a seething undertow of brewing insecurity, of a confidence frail. At a whiff of weakness, and with bated breath, both men and women alike are ready to carve you up, gnaw at your core and spit you out all in a blink of an eyelid.

The male of species is no less discriminatory, be it a man or a woman as victim... In their eyes they are of equal prey. Women however tend to bully their own, as statistics are convinced it is about 70 percent of the time. They are not largesse of spirit, of compassion, of mercy...rather feigning ignorance as their defense mechanism ...Self- reliance has never screeched more sharply.

As a society tightly bound by the sense of homogeneity; the 'Island' mentality as it were, here does not welcome the new, does not encourage the different, has very little interest in the other, *unless* it is to appropriate, to assimilate and to serve the purpose of cultural aggrandizement.

Window-dressing the reality cannot sustain itself. The image perfect slips, the frailty of the system, wrought with inconsistencies is revealed. To the naked eye, the visitor does not detect the ripples of malaise fermenting.

The public façade is a polished surface of sheen, attractive and inviting. Yet with time, the circumstances shift, the mood darkens, the sullen pangs of deep-seeded antagonism lift its ugly head. You do not belong, nor are you made to feel a part of this society...ah *gaijin kirai* ...hate foreigners (!) constantly mumbled beneath their breath...yes, even today.

Solipsism of a nation, oh what extravagance, a complete reveling in extreme egocentrism.

Could that be at all possible? Excessive occupation with identity as a collective, not that of the individual *per se* in the conventional sense, but an almost vainglorious obsession in upholding appearances, for the sake of what is right or just....the dilemma of a herd mentality. Blinded by the sway of dominance, who becomes the moderator of such cultivation? Ah yes, the Bastion of Standards and Compliancy of all that is quasi quixotic in endeavors, yes, the executive powers of harmony and conformity.

Communally homespun, of sophistication lacking, of base tribal, that of a mobbing mentality.

The character of the individual becomes the target, is ostracized for not kowtowing to the group, tormented and cursed for their differences, and made to feel victim in this world.

It starts off in their youngsters, and extends right up to their elders, the notion of bullying their peers so as to instill order and fear. We see it in the playground, refusing to share toys, as well as the exclusion in games. The adults have not grown out of such antics at play, perhaps part of their DNA some may say... The business world too is tainted so, an extreme form of control perpetrating the system, fomenting subservience, of pandering to the fold. Outliers be aware...yours is not a position to take. For you will be shamed for your adroitness and punished thus, a refusal to come back to the fray, ah the unlucky ones.

And with this frailty of mind, society in general acts like the petulant child in the sandbox, relational aggression occasionally frothing above the surface.

This assault of sensibility, though not isolated to those living here I must admit, stems from the desperation to persevere despite the choking restrictions, preserve the given, iron out any wrinkles, smother ambition... all codified principles set in stone. Even to step outside the accepted, not so much rebel against the system, is discouraged, no *faux pas* be made in the milieu of the public realm, for the common good, coercion is not directed in that way...no, the attack is more personal, of the individual.

Take for instance the workplace environment, where, have you believe, a married woman, becomes pregnant. She is politely asked to step aside, either leave by the back door or face indignity from her peers. Not only men tend to harass the mother- to- be, she is also the brunt of beatings from her fellow *sisters*...justifying their reactions of not being fair, out of irritation, of the demands of the workload surmounting or out of plain jealousy, sadly.

How this playground before me plays havoc with the mind.

Never before has such tainting and taunting especially among the 'weaker' folk been of mine (now I appreciate the label!)

As is my daily routine, travelling through the center of Tokyo, I never fail to meet the innuendo, the cattiness, the disparaging remarks, all in a whisper's breath, an earshot of my presence.

In twos and threes, they gossip among themselves, for reasons I am the center of *their* attention, I do not know!

And who are these people anyway?

Not one of them I know by name.

And yet the badgering and baiting continues today, you would think after all this time, another victim would be their prey.

Don't be so sensitive, I hear you say.

For the last twenty it has been the case.

Yes, the spirit has faltered, but the mind has not fallen to the character assassinations, even on a daily basis.

Maybe I should count myself lucky.

At least I am not persecuted for the color of my skin, nor religious beliefs, ...how much should one put up with?

The female *bitch*, a terribly apt term to carry, attacks with the fury no less an animal. Perpetrating the scourge of the victim, none other than a sister, this unleashing much harder to investigate, and difficult to gauge. For it is not a bloody nose we can trace as proof, nothing of the physical damage can be assumed. It is the emotional scars that are left bleeding, the pus oozing not being easily sealed. No! This is conspiratorial; of spreading rumors, wicked backstabbing, social exclusion, savage character baiting of an insidious nature.

How do you shield yourself from such menacing threats verbal and offensive? The logical frame would be to steer ahead regardless. Although shaken, the staying power of the individual learns to resist and assumes a strategy of self-preservation, of defense.

Life, just like a lottery, is the gamble you take. Roll the dice, and see what fortune waits. None of us are ever immune to such cruelty of life's permutations, we take the good with the bad, and leave it at that. Yet among the harbored and well armored, not one among you would champion forces of terror, so caught up in the defense of your own self-centered narrative. Not one among you could offer an olive branch of peace, your callousness stripped of any spirit altruistic, leaves this impression shallow and frightening.

As a woman guided by faith, I learnt to listen and not judge in haste. My education and beliefs may run contrary, and remain so even today, never were they a deliberate attempt to destabilize the social order of the day...I am but one, how could that be my intention, why would it be so?

I refuse to be pressured into cowering to a society whose system of cohesion and uniformity is suffocating the very essence of human nature...that freedom to express, and hold opinion, to voice reason, and challenge authority.

The pricks and jabs may sting, but it will never rock the core of my convictions. I do not need to stand proud, my footing remains firm, the will to survive unfazed.

Often mistakenly classified as one and the same, if we consider the two cultures that of Japanese and South Korean for instance, a rift clearly divides the principles governing such societies with histories dating back centuries. For in the eye of the Japanese, the fundamentals of *wa* hold supreme, above and beyond the concepts of truth and morality, as measured and motioned as well established. More akin with the systems Western, the Koreans lean more on the fundamentals of rules governing the order of principles. To determine the essence of character would be, in Japan among peers convened and deemed, evaluating the relative worth according to *his* standing. For the Korean say, the law would abide, demarcating any further discussion on the value or *his* pride.

Letter 4:

What must it be like sitting on the ocean at night...the wind pressing against your face...the universe lit with stars...it must be a serene wonder...but for you it is your job!

To have that moment with the wonders of the universe must truly be magical...I remember my dive safaris...watching the stars in amazement...and realizing how small we really are in this vast and crazy world...yet here we are...two people meeting for the first time... oceans apart, worlds away yet somehow connected...

You have brought a feeling of warmth and comfort to my world, opening up my mind to the endless possibilities that await...where we go from here nobody knows, why we are here cannot be explained...I am only grateful for the day you reached out and said 'hello.'

I want you to know me better, as I do of you...no pressure...this will take time. What I do recognize is this mutual affection developing, a fondness for communication, an eagerness to get to know each other... patience being the factor testing our commitment...I long for the day we can meet face to face...to lock eyes and physically connect...

You have pierced my heart with your words of love...and I am about to collapse in my seat...you have unnerved my spirit ...I can hardly breathe...I want to see, be with near you, touch you...

How do I love thee? Can I match the same fortitude of spirit, the lust for life, the unbridled love you express? This is a challenge I know none other...I am willing to reciprocate on a level beyond comprehension... trembling in my fears of wonder...take me on that journey of exchange... you are holding my heart in your hand...and lead me forward...I can but follow...feeling lost for so long...you have arrived at my side, and are now taking the lead... engulfed in this brilliant light you emanate, this burning glow of joy I am in love...there is nothing else to describe it ....you have mesmerized my sense of being beyond control...you have fully embraced my soul...and as I sit, regaining my breath I am convinced this is meant to be, that this is so....

You are the key unlatching passion I have never known...Fearless in your trust, I am only bowled over in your willingness to share your honesty...I am truly blessed.

You have triggered in me a confidence to love you, an unleashing of liberty to express my true feelings, natural and uninhibited...I have never been this struck by anyone quite like you in my life! You have strengthened my conviction in believing that love does really exist, for the right person, at the right time...For you are my only channel of emotional refuge, where I feel safe and secure knowing you are there.

Each passing day only strengthens these seeds of this flourishing relationship... I love you!

OH MOTHER!

The power of the mother figure: the life-giving bearer, burdened by child-birth, the bloodline of the family.

And mine? How do I describe her? A hard nut to crack indeed! A pious woman of Catholic persuasion, she remains a devoted member of the congregation. Without fail every Sunday morning, to church service, mass, her only real outlet in the suburban environs.

A woman of narrow frame, petite in stature, she managed to bear four girls, I, being the elder. How my mother coped is beyond me still. Her health quickly depleted over the stresses of delivering her litter. Every fiber of her body drained of any reserves of energy, why she was to have so many, was baffling, and can only be deduced by the pressures of being a good Catholic.

Serving the church was her contribution to society…or was it? Delving into the many layers of history I was to learn, in my early twenties, of the very existence of depression present in my mother's life. Torn away from her own mother not long after birth, taken custody by her father, she and her sister were conveniently shuttled off, and raised in a convent. With her younger sister the two were cloistered in this monastic environment governed by the sisters superior, uniformed, corseted and veiled completely; a whole other listing of issues which won't be analyzed here. How that played on her upbringing I will never fully realize, though I surmise it would skewer the picture of a stable family environment.

How was she to know the love of a mother? How was she to transfer a sense of love to her daughters… without recognizing it herself?

The solution to any problems, it seemed, was to seek advice from the church, so naturally Grandad took this as the ticket to salvation. Poor woman, subjugated to the forces ever powerful, she knew none other but to obey without question. Faith was her rock, her foundation, her core. Spiritually her convictions lay in God the father, the holy mother, her faith resolute, I have known no other.

Perhaps her remedy it was advocated, she should marry and have babies… this would save her. Adhering to such advice, no literally, she would follow blindly the authority, devout supremely. Under the guidance of counsellors then: the doctors, the priests and other professionals… of course mostly men. Mind you predominately male in persuasion, they would pontificate on the duties of a mother, her need to procreate, of being a solid role model, contributing to the greater good of society.

As a Catholic married to an Italian, very much influenced by the Church's principles; of familial duty and societal responsibility, a family prized in the conservative circles of tradition…as the sole function of any union of marriage.

Was she up to it? Physically she could just manage. Having had two miscarriages before I arrived on the *scene*, surely indicated the frailty of her genes. Yet three more were to follow within a span of ten years.

We four girls were a healthy tribe of youngsters, getting up to mischief like any kid growing up in the suburbs. The frequent conflicts, the bickering and trouble too soon developed once an awareness of fairness could be manoeuvred. 'She has more, I have less,' tended to be the gauge of balance. And how we fought! Screaming matches would leave my father inadequate. Indisposed he would resort to the garage where he would tinker away at his latest contraptions, a resting place, a moment of peace. He, the youngest of six boys and two girls, a big Italian family, he was inept at handling emotional young women. He tried to compensate dearly with efforts of understanding, his love more apparent than I have ever expressed appreciation.

As teenagers life would prove more difficult for my parents, the demands of young women, the need for protection. The crisis of identity, the physical transformations, the mental anguish of not being understood, as well as the constant conflicts of opinion, did not make this a happy home. There was always some worry, some issue, another problem unresolved.

I remember sitting after dinner at the table, my mother completely drained from doing all the chores of the day, which was normally the case, us girls way too pre-occupied to help out (to my dismay.) Another catfight was brewing from the living room, between the two younger, not sure exactly, perhaps over the television channel or program, anyway…

Lamenting her lot for the first time ever I can recall, I must have been thirteen at the time, I will never forget the words that were uttered, 'I should never have had the youngest, you know.' Feeling perplexed, I was fraught with confusion, how could a mother be brought to saying such a thing was hard to swallow.

Four to the brood would satisfy expectations…It was a terrible burden emotionally for her; she was not ready for the role as prescribed her. This was, in *their* eyes, an antidote (albeit temporary) for her own misguided perceptions of who she was in society; her role in life. How could a mother deny the life of her own child? 'She shouldn't have had her,' still rings in my head, and has stuck with me even today.

On reflection, perhaps my perception has shifted yet at that time I had no grasp of such an admission. Obviously the pressures of being a mother were way too demanding for this poor woman, who frankly should never had so many from the outset.

Do you now see why I was turned off having children even at such a young age? The coping mechanisms depleted, of a trapped and isolated individual, cut-off from society with limited means of communication. Her partner, like mine, a non- native speaker; belonging to a culture no less diverse and conflicting of values as my very own predicament features.

I was, and perhaps even today, a re-incarnation of 'her' and hated admitting this undeniable truth. My sisters would joke how alike we were in nature, and quickly saw the similarities of character, of behavior. Yes, I quietly recoiled in protest; I desperately needed to seek the antithesis of all that, the life of hers had been advised, there was little choice I detected, that of a victim of her time. I was not to be trapped into suffering the way she did…The anguish, the burden carried for so long exasperated her physical condition, all bottled up, no venting of frustrations, she in her pious devotion, would bear her cross as her duty of religious observance.

I have never had a desire to give birth, have children or felt the need to fulfill my duties as an *upright* citizen, as a wife and mother.

In the passage of time, of growing up, exploration and discovery of the other sex, would naturally play a role in shaping my character. Coming from a predominantly all female home environment, as already mentioned, very little contact with boys was apparent. The male of gender was nothing more than a distant curiosity, an oddity. They exist, I acknowledged, they are here on this planet; be kind, and show some tolerance!

Being the first born, I felt it important to appease the expectations of my parents. Very aware of social pressures, I struggled with the frustrations bubbling under the surface. Disconnected culturally, the problems of identity, was I even Australian? With an Anglo-Saxon leaning, blended with Mediterranean stock, what was my position in the overall realm of this narration?

Communicating such tensions was virtually non- existent; very few outlets for venting or vexing were prevalent. We belonged to family was my father's mentality, so essentially nothing else was relevant.

Often we met the extended family on my father's side; the numerous uncles, aunts, cousins, nephews and nieces, all of us gathering for celebrations as customs, as ceremonies making the *festa* in the Italian spirit much more pertinent for identity. The welcoming aroma from the kitchen permeating the house of my *nonna,* it was the food; the sharing of a meal, of enjoying, of eating, basic pleasures in life. Any excuse for a celebration; the essence of the Italians…a wonderful, happy, healthy outlook on life….

Pivotal to the cohesion of this union, the matriarch, a woman left widowed for most of her life, wore, every day I knew her, the black dress of bereavement. Speaking no English we tried to connect, using gestures, making eye contact, relying on instinct as the only bet. Confusing to some, as kids we accepted, this was our life, there was nothing needed changing.

It was an environment embracing, yet strangely foreign. We belonged as children of my father, yet we couldn't follow a word on offer. Failing to comprehend fully their ways, this is what set us apart, we were of a different nature. A sense of dislocation despite efforts, impressed upon me at an early age that we were not quite the same.

Letter 5:

You are in my every thought, above and beyond the mundane of life... You are the magnet drawing me closer and pushing me forward to you...You are the shining beam of brilliance, guiding my heart in the ordinary of the everyday...you have revealed to me a vison of light and beauty...

This is what I am prepared to do for love...

To run to the ends of the world with you, pack up everything here and follow you my love...

Hedging all bets, I am ready to go, and leave behind this world I have grown fond of, albeit a challenging one on many levels. It has taken me until now several years to establish in this islolating and closed existence in Japan...but it too has been rewarding....my students have become my friends, a support network I will forever be in their debt...

Any yet the divine tug of your love edges me towards something greater, something I have never known, but recognize as just as important in existence...finding a soul mate who I want to dedicate my love of life with, my passion with, my world...

This is a huge step to take... to pack up everything and just go... but this is where I find myself with you Wesley...promise me this is what you want from me...

To do so, I would be totally dependent on you, for the first phase of my existence... I would need to adjust to this new environment, and figure out a way to contribute to you, to society in general....I want to give my all, and must recognize in what capacity favorable...

Am I a fool to rush into this? For I have known no other...I am wanting to give up everything I have here and follow you...is this madness, is love blind...I cannot answer these questions...

In my mind's eye, my gut feeling, my instinct tells me to go...and venture forward with this man I hardly know, a man who keeps pledging his love for me, who dedicates his waking hours to convince me that this is the right path to choose.

I stand at this cross roads in my life, and today have a clearer picture of what I want... I want you! How am I to know whether this is right? At this point I can only gauge from my impressions of you, the words of love you exchange, the constant dedication to our blossoming relationship, the passionate magnet of your love edging me toward you like none other... am I reading this clearly, is that what you want, my dear Wesley?

STUCK BETWEEN A ROCK
AND A HARD PLACE

Ah…Japan…the *exotic* far east…

Certainly far-flung, the surroundings less than extravagant, a richer tapestry paraded in my travels to places like India, so too had the weird, wonderful and fantastic in the more remote corners of the globe. No, this was a dated description, of a time when few were privileged to travel, of voyaging the great oceans on sailing ships, the likes of *Titanic* come to mind….even south of the border was painted with this same stroke of the unfamiliar!

Anyway, in my predicament, any perceptions of the exotic, a mere disillusion, quickly faded. I was holed up in a suburb, living in a two-room apartment no bigger than my bedroom when growing up….no literally! Cramped, dark, and dank, this was to be considered 'home' for a few years at least.

Having spent a time a vegetarian, I remained circumspect about venturing carnivore. Not completely adverse though I must admit, but not overly enthusiastic either….it was to be a gradual conversion over an extended period…. With such sensitivity one would wonder why I decided to live above a meat shop, a butcher's…where the daily routine of barbequing flesh became part of the morning ritual…sacrifices to the gods… so to speak.

Regardless of the circumstances, I was determined to carve my way, to welcome the opportunities that waited, deal with the pitfalls come what may. I had made a choice; I was resolute in believing I wanted to be here and, if anything, learn from a culture far removed from my own.

How naïve had I been!

Back home in Oz, a friendly greeting would most often be reciprocated with a response… Hello, how are you today? Fine, and you…a commonplace, simple exchange….no ties attached, no obligations, no burdens or duress…an ease very natural and quaintly neighborly.

The day the tables were turned, a stab of reality puncture my cloud of innocence (or was it naivety,) was at *that* coffee shop close to the station. An older suburb, with a few run-down drab looking family businesses, a green grocer's, day laborers' canteen, bookshop, and bakery, I found a place serving what was a semblance of 'coffee' (the Italians would shake their head in horror and cry *Che diavolo è questo???: what the hell is this?*)… …weak drip filter was served. I had not much option but to make that selection, nothing else resembled anything remotely like an *espresso* I was so fond of back home.

It was lunchtime and busy with the local office workers, a few humble operations in the area…mostly poorly signed and indistinct. In the congestion I found a seat, another vacant adjacent. Then suddenly and swiftly this character appeared. How I didn't notice him beforehand is beyond me. Tall of stature, a bit more stocky than the average here, this guy had bright auburn hair, a box perm close to the scalp, whose eyes were a glaring blue from the contacts I assume, and dressed in a more flamboyant outfit… why am I not surprised!

Without hesitation, unlike the majority here, he approached and asked in coherent Italian whether the seat was taken and would I mind him sitting next to me. Surprisingly I had not expected to hear my father's tongue being uttered…in Japan it was predominately Japanese, or a bastardized version of *Ingurish*, (though admittedly they do try!) Upon hearing such tones familiar, I was bemused, and curious…who was he? And how could he assume that I understood the language?

Naturally I was obliging, and welcomed the company. Not knowing anyone in the area, it was a pleasant diversion relating to someone in a language mutually conversant with, or so it seemed. The repartee transpiring felt awkward, not to mention the surrounding patrons prying, as they do in these parts of the wood, monitoring and marking mental notes though how many really understood Italian I could hardly estimate….very few I suspect. It appeared the skills were limited, the questions falling blank, the artifice quickly revealing the shoddy nature of this exchange.

E voila! I was being duped…and for what reason?

For a time no less than six months, this clown would stalk me. He, being unemployed and of dubious mental stability, would watch me from a distance, enter the community center where I taught, and wait until closing. The wide reception bay was from ceiling to floor, glass paneled; the fellow teachers and I would joke about it being a fish bowl. This was no laughing matter...fully exposed, the flotsam and jetsam passing on the street would peer in, "those pesky foreigners what havoc and corruption they are causing"...so exposed, so vulnerable.

I would ride my bicycle as this is the preferred form of mobility; it makes sense, there are so many crammed in a concentrated area, the roads resemble more laneways, ingrained shortcuts crisscrossing the landscape. For me, being a complete stranger to the neighborhood, I would follow the major routes (no.1 to be precise.) And nearly every night the white Toyota sedan would follow, the muffler's drone amplifying the tension...heavy and foreboding... 'don't give him the attention he craves, look straight ahead,' was my mantra most evenings. Occasionally I would drop by the convenience store to grab something for dinner, *lo and behold*, he would appear, sometimes parked at the entrance or in the store. 'Ignore him, focus,' at once the panic would set in... my heart racing, my head blurred with confusion....what could I do?

On my way up the hill to where I lived, a steep one garland with cherry blossom trees arching both sides of the road, rather pretty in spring admittedly, the constant drone would bellow...god he is still here....I would rush indoors, lock as fast as possible and wait for him to leave. I knew he hadn't...again the car was a dead give- away...not so crafty nor strategic.

To be honest he never physically approached.

Letter 6:

You are a sky full of stars...lighting up a path so clear I can but follow...

The magnitude of your presence, even at this remote distance, leaves me mesmerized...you have pierced my heart and I am left yearning to see you grows with each passing day...my head fills with questions what if..., it couldn't be ....but it is...I must accept that the love you express is genuine and real...I believe in you Wesley...I may appear vulnerable and weak...I have fallen for a guy I don't really know...and it is only through this connection you have convinced me that love exists,...and is true.

I give you my heart, I give you my soul...that is what I can offer in this exchange...I want to keep giving... there is no turning back...You have lit a fire in the depths of my belly, and how it burns for you...every time we connect heat rises from below...and a warm glow in my heart reminds me once again you are near....I love the impact you have made on me...turning me on like this, awakening my soul...and unnerving my spirit so much so I remain nervous and excited overwhelmed...

I had never thought this uniting of souls could ever be possible... you have plucked at my heart strings...and now a beautiful harmony unfolds...you are an angel sent from above...how this is possible...I cannot make sense of this...you are a man among men...a gentle giant with fortitude of spirit...daring and willing to traipse half way round the world in your quest for love...mercy upon me...I pray you won't be disappointed...for I am a simple being with basic needs... with a renewed conviction instilled by you that love exists and is true....I want to believe!

Until that day we meet face to face, I hold onto your every word, every gesture expressed...having faith in you, recognizing that we are beginning to mirror each other in our feelings, in our goals convinces me that this is real...I have nothing to turn back on, I have a glowing vision of a future...and am drawn to it like nothing before...the light emitting is blinding I know, but it warm and beautiful...that being you, my dear Wesley.

UTSUBYO: DEPRESSION

The repressive nature of humans is a debilitating condition to fathom. Why we burden ourselves with such indulgences is a symptom of our madness. We bring it upon ourselves, a mechanism deceptively menacing, playing havoc with our outlook, and our feelings.

The ancient Greeks knew a thing or two, about recognizing the damaging effects of 'bottling it up' all inside. This would adversely affect the stasis of condition, turning against itself, and triggering negativity. It was one of the revered forefathers of ancient Greece, dear Aristotle who proclaimed the need for **catharsis** as a means of channeling any grief, of alleviating the mounting tensions within. As responsible for the reinterpretation, the purging of mind without inhibition as therapy was prescribed to the young and old.

Tragic plays at the *amphitheatre* were performed, were experienced by the punters, prying open a whole spectrum of *pathos* to unfurl. Like laundry hanging out to the elements, from anger, sadness and guilt, such afflictions all vulnerable in the public arena, inflamed the tensions from their inner sanctums. And just like that, brought relief to the masses, realigning the sense of balance in our overall condition.

It must be known a few centuries later, Sigmund Freud would uphold the cathartic benefits of the clinic's sofa.

In my first place of employment, I was hired to *teach* English at a community center....yes, the word teach is italicized, emphasizing the very dubious nature of my role. We would sit, for a consultation so to speak, oftentimes the single student and I in a private room dimly lit, cozy but not your typical classroom; none of the hardware, so to speak, in sight. Those students enrolled were mostly from around there, housewives with neither work commitments nor hobbies other than 'Ingurish,' a handful of men, some retired, others holding responsibilities unconventional, and some high school students, who would pop in for their 'five-minutes- with- the- foreigner' experience.

We would commence with a light warm-up as you do, to create a relaxed atmosphere for these mostly nervous, highly strung individuals, so preoccupied with their hemmed in existence. Little interest was shown in fine-tuning the skills as the fundamentals of grammar had already been covered in their six years of foreign language schooling. Very little was made to improve ... no, this was a session for venting....of addressing the hardships faced in their personal lives; the problems of their never- at -home husbands, the wonders of alcohol, the gossiping on their neighbors, the problems with the young generation today...all in all an opportunity to air personal griefs, never before done for fear of social shame.

Fear of slipping socially speaking; as in the case of being considered depressive, (what would the neighbors think!) has forced such individuals to seek shelter; incidentally in the privacy of a foreigner, all in the name of practicing English conversation; for surreptitiously this arrangement would draw less attention to the burgeoning angst surfacing, and safely within the confines of the classroom environment verbalizing such woes would commence.

Lives lived separately, the extended periods of silence, only conjure up an image of dislocation... of not fully integrating, the dread of being rejected. It is agonized the world over, periodically in stages; man's quest for survival, upon reflection, his navel-gazing. The deeper the absorption, the darker the perception, to a point where this world becomes a harsh and hostile environment...For it takes effort and fortitude of spirit to ride on this current of life....to stand with conviction and confront....yet sadly we *wee* mortals are pained to believe, this is not possible....and so we yield to the dark side of nature.

Incidentally seeing a psychologist was never entertained back then, and I suppose not even now for the same issues of keeping up appearances. And I, despite the few years of employment, presented myself as qualified and somewhat experienced in the field of teaching English as a second language, now had to perform the role of the advisor, nurturer, psychologist and friend. This was not part of my training, nor was I particularly interested in functioning on such levels, yet felt it my duty to fulfill the obligations of my employment...and so I stayed.

At first these 'counsellings' revealed to me, an insight into the ordinary lives of these people, the majority being of the post-baby boomer generation. They had lived through *the bubble;* an economic miracle, reveled in the joys of affluence and tasted a sense of power, of entitlement in the world. Yet something was amiss, they were not a happy bunch. Not like the Thais with whom I got to know, and live among for a brief period. No, these encounters reflected the given environment; hidden, dark and brooding.

What transpired brought me no closer to comprehending the magnitude of their society's modern-day woes, but it made me realize there were some very bitter and twisted people co-existing in the system, which on first impression, seemed so orderly and mildly mannered, so tolerant of others, and community-minded. How these private rants proved contrary to my initial perception... instilling a society more vitriolic than caring, disgruntled than forgiving, misanthropic than kind hearted...where was I?

Letter 7:

You move me in ways inconceivable, and there is no control... I am growing madly in love with a man I have but an exchange of words to rely on...

I want to fulfill your needs, and bring you happiness to the ends of this planet. I want your daughter to love me too, as she will play a most important role in the balance of this relationship...Not having children I cannot claim confidence in such matters but having been surrounded by younger sisters at home, as well as teaching I can only welcome this next chapter in my life...being a positive and strong role model to our daughter...

You are offering me all this, a huge turn around in my life but one I embrace with outstretched arms...I welcome the challenges this new life brings, realizing deep in my soul, it is all for love.

I want for you to be truly happy Wesley...at times it will be a guessing game gauging what is too much, and what is not enough... but these are the trials we can attest...I want to know what you like, what you prefer, and what you detest...

You have invited me into your world, and already I feel welcomed and loved....this I do not take for granted as I have known none other...I have longed to be genuinely apart of something for a very long time, to be accepted and respected...you have already laid down such foundations...I am blessed.

I want to touch the highest peaks with you, dive the deepest oceans with you, sail the roughest seas, and be pulled this way and that, because my love for you will remain unshaken...I am determined to keep it so...and if by chance it slips, there will be ways of re-igniting the flame...let our imaginations go wild... let freedom reign...exploring every possibility as if it were the last option available...our adventure into the great unknown has yet begun...

Stop me if we become a couple whose conversation runs dry...life is precious, we only live once...I want to grasp it with my two hands, holding you and Deborah, and run freely through God's slice of heaven... our life together...love knows no boundaries...I truly believe this is the case hence my need to pack up and leave...for this vision of tomorrow awaits... God bless you Wesley...

It wasn't meant to be like this...

In more conservative circles we pre-determine our future in earnest, to a society esteemed we aspire, to sit among those in the right circles; keeping up with the *Joneses* or rather the *Hondas* one could say. If we adhere to such precedents our forefathers tread, and follow tradition, we won't veer off course and get lost in the melee of life.

Being human, for the most part we are attracted by what stimulates us, triggered by desire, motivated by the very lack of that something, however the definition.

Mine is not any more unique; it is a story to be told, a warning to others, a chapter of reality rarely uncovered.

How did I end up here I find it difficult to fathom….perhaps in working back through the recent course of events may clarify the bewilderment lingering.

This is not a love song

The marriage, like some I surmise, after a while turned sour.

A mixed marriage, I had moved from my country Australia in the vain hope of uncovering life's mysteries waiting in the big wide world. That world ended up being Japan…both literally and metaphorically the antithesis of anything of such scale…

Travel had been my outlet, my escape from the dreary, and somewhat pained home environ. I wanted a release, a way out….and the stimulus of experiencing the other, the exotic, the old and cultured feeding my mind, breathing life into my soul.

An exchange student in the west of France: Angouleme with its vineyards, wineries, and traditions spanning over centuries, far beyond the chapters recent of the land *down under*, naturally I was captivated to learn more, to bear witness to the wonders and beauty of other worlds, of lives entirely different from my own.

This desire to discover brought me to some less trodden paths, more formidable conditions, spiritually uplifting and ultimately rewarding encounters never imagined in my most ambitious hours. For it was the people who shaped such a vision, in some cases life-altering experiences. (I could go on about such characters who affected me in such a way today but that would mean another story be written, and meandering down that path takes a lot of time and energy.)

I am to focus on what brought me here...and why the path chosen was decided....how did it all end up like this?

Back to the marriage, I an Australian, and he a *Nippon- jin:* Japanese.... there I have stated the blinking obvious....two universes in complete opposition attempting, in hindsight perhaps, to bridge cultures and misconceptions. We were no soldiers valiantly upholding the guard, proving to society, that yes, peace and understanding can coexist in a world misguided by populism, bigotry, in a word narrow mindedness.

We were in effect two kids trying to understand each other...prepared to give it a go.

A predominantly conservative society still developing in its pluralism, in its maturity...not yet ripened. In emotional intimacy too, this is sadly yet at an embryonic stage; especially when it comes to love. Not in the sense of paternal love, nor that of platonic love, neither that of patriotic love...all heavily charged tenets of the culture firmly cementing the minds, and hearts of society here....

No!

We are talking about passion, arousal, chemically- charged, heart wrenching desire, very rarely demonstrated, very rarely addressed, with quite as much openness or acceptance as in the west...to embrace, to share and enjoy, to satisfy... (what do you mean you don't hear them at it... the walls here are so thin!)

A condition so prevalent it is affecting the nation, hindering the future of the Japanese population. In media speak it is coined as so: *sekkusu shinai shokogun,* or "celibacy syndrome."

What might that mean for the uninitiated? It is a condition, often by choice, of refraining from forming any intimate relationship, let alone one based on love. Romantic coupling is, quite literally, of a dying breed, here anyway so the statistics reveal. The survey of 2011 shows 61% of unmarried men and 49% of women aged 18-34 had no interest romantically or otherwise. In addition, a third of people under 30, had never dated and was most probably still living under the roof of their parents. Incidentally, a rise of almost 10% from five years earlier, marks this trend in society bordering on a national problem.

Reserved and retiring, temporal pleasures only entertained…like that of cherry blossom…fleeting moments yes, the yen somewhat tepid, reflective of mood, of character, of season…fleeting moments but once in a while…

Guarded, formal and sadly hidden from public scrutiny, for fear of being frowned upon by their neighbors, by not meeting expectations, the bond coveted beyond recognition….appearances never meant so much….

A report uncovered not long ago, best supporting the focus on love lost in this world. A Japanese variety show had devised an experiment. Their purpose was to highlight the differences between two cultures: Japanese and South Korean. Presented on the program were two panels of five women. The set up was simple: each woman was to phone her husband and state matter-of–fact how she loved him. From the Japanese there was little variation in the responses given: 'Are you OK? '… 'You must be drunk,' laughing and dismissive. Sadly only one on the panel from the Japanese side could reciprocate a reply reflective of the sentiment intimated.

To look at the responses from the Korean side, was rather baffling for the audience of the home front. When receiving the very same message of love from their wives, they stated without shame, of how they love their spouses, even very much in some cases. Scenes captured for broadcasting purposes, highlighted this fact of being at ease at showing their affection in an honest and public fashion: of simply holding hands, kissing and cuddling, endearing gestures made open, how liberated! The Koreans have learnt that romance should not be denied, nor smothered by the precepts of societal guidelines. It is only a matter of attitude and conviction to naturally accept; life is worth loving, loving is worth life.

Do we find the same in Japan? Very few traces are sighted. This reluctance to express openly is perhaps conflicting with culture, I surmise. A stubborn resistance to deny natural urges is sensed, all for the sake of what is 'appropriate behavior.' Woe betide if caught pecking your wife, the laughing stock in the office for the rest of your life!

Co-habitation…co-habiting….living together….but really?

Two beings existing under the same roof, for what purpose, for what reason? Never meeting eye to eye, rarely interacting, just being …under the guise of a happily married couple. No goals, no purpose, just surviving for the sake of the proverbial sanctimonious union…

A mixed one at that…culturally speaking or did I mean to say mixed up?

In the eyes of convention, no less prevalent than here in Japan, the marriage of two houses, two families publicly demonstrating acceptance and approval, this bond very rarely defined by love….a *modern* and often trivial factor in the equation. Ironic really, given the fact Shakespeare had scripted so fine a tale at the end of the 16th century; the epitome of man's tragic quest...

O ROMEO, ROMEO, WHEREFORE ART THOU ROMEO?

For many years now, it was the role of the parents, to influence the arrangement of setting up a marriage. All business-like in pretense, this institution was observed, to do away with the emotionally driven lusts of a post-pubescent youth. To fix a partnership compatible and rational, clear-headed choices were of the command of the elder folk. None of the charm of character nor physical attraction were of consideration, the future prospects of a well- educated doctor, lawyer, politician were determinants.

For the Westerner, particularly of the more liberal and widely embracing in the catholic sense, romantic notions have tainted our system, our culture, our existence. Permeating throughout the ages, is man's endeavors to epitomize such affliction of desire. Touching all facets of life, this need to express love in its mellifluous tones of beauty; to depict, to capture the passion burning within, such poetry existing since man's yearning of love unrequited.

It is sadly withdrawn from such circles here. Commitment to a partner considered more of a burden, of drudgery so it appears. The costs, oh my, of entertaining an engagement let alone one of romantic inclination, leads such people to be singularly shallow and vacuous.

Pressure of meeting the expectations of the in-laws,

Of producing off-spring and continuing lineage;

What a hassle for 'my own selfish endeavors.'

A quote of statistics from Japan's Institute of Population and Social Security shows an overwhelmingly high proportion of young women failing to aspire to being married. The prospects of finding the one, is of fruitless ambition,….a life celibate, of a lifetime single tends to be more appealing these days. 'What is wrong with this?' I hear her say.

This need for independence, of breaking with tradition, has meant for women this push to shift the balance. Not as pronounced some would hope, but a stance is taken to hold a choice rupturing the given order; outright refusal to follow the established course.

Society is not what it was. No longer is life time employment guaranteed, prospects of promotion looking slim, the Japanese men slipping in their drive to get ahead poses little hope for their wee brides-to-be.

What chance does a woman have of finding and trapping that Prince charming, of not having to work, of having a healthy pay package, covering the costs of going to the *estee: aesthetic salons, nailists: manicurists*, and hair salon, not to mention a nice car, private education for the littlies, of being the envy of most. This is but a figment of her imagination, maybe in a different period, of her mother's generation. He no longer provides such lofty expectations, the range of choice squeezes narrow, why, give up of course!

Forging ahead women are gaining traction, keeping a career ahead of marriage. For the options that are put forward, are as an unattractive minefield of choice. Yet conservative attitudes remain solid, of the workplace and of the home.

The duty of the wife is to remain in the conventional sense, to look after her husband and be a good housewife. Balancing both in this day and age, means forfeiting aspirations of comfort, for a life less appealing, the burden of parenthood, of a life becoming less affordable, certainly does not render much hope in the future of their survival as a nation, the demographics of a society. Even the option of the *un*conventional; of cohabiting or unwed parenthood is still frowned upon by many and dogged by the disapproval of the bureacratics.

The strangeness of a foreign wife, the anomaly breaking with convention.... what trouble she would bring! The wild wayward western woman...please don't upset the delicate fabric of society far- extending beyond the matrimonial suite! Veiled in tradition, imbued in values beyond the intimate and personal, monitored by the purveyors of good taste; the surveyor, conveyor, gainsayer and portrayer...'The Bastion of Standards and Compliancy'...how does the modern woman adjust!

'A gaijin': foreigner...oh that must be tricky.

For social elevation, privilege or career?

It is said some people get into a relationship simply because they believe it can advance their status.

What had I succumbed to?

I learnt to persevere, to preserve my precious self and persist...

Survival meant committing to a routine whereby I gained a sense of control, an avoidance of being dominated, of sharing in what *he* wanted to do or society upholds.

I would get up early at 4:30 a.m. to visit the gym. The reasons are three-fold: One, I didn't want to play the dutiful housewife and prepare a boxed lunch *bento* as was expected. Besides my cooking wasn't satisfying enough to him, lacking... how do you say, mother's sauces as custom...Two, I had my own work schedule which was quite demanding, the first lesson starting at 8:00. And most importantly, fitness was the essence to my endurance...I needed to be strong, mentally and physically.

Why did I bother investing in such a lifestyle.....there was very little choice. I was a foreign woman isolated from her own, ostracized for her differences, vulnerable to the forces existing.

As for making friends of the same age or gender just does not readily happen in this society...the stigma attached to associating with a foreigner poses a conundrum with most of the 'insular kind' here.

.....*those* people bring trouble and upset *our* delicate balance maintained, preserved over the centuries.....

We were to cruise for a time, oblivious to the social pressures, lost in our world, naive and innocent. Not of convention, how could it be, two cultures colliding, we were not 'in love' but were prepared to invest in this prospect of love.

Very rare for a foreigner, especially a woman, to partner a local lad, the very thought stirring shockwaves of great magnitude, rocking any semblance of order, of core values, the very foundation of establishment here.

Was I your 'social' experiment, here to entertain you?

Certainly a curiosity, this relationship was riddled with misperceptions nominally cultural since its inception, unbeknown to naïve me.

The few ex-patriot women encountered had all met their partners overseas, such awareness of the 'other' easing some of the misconceptions of the cultural barriers, beyond the shores of *Yamato*. (It would appear Chinese, Korean, and Japanese scribes regularly wrote *Wa* or *Yamato* "Japan" with the Chinese character 倭 until the 8th century.)

How was this even possible?

A local fascinated, then taking the plunge, running the gamut and finally proposing all within a seven-year incubation…unconventional indeed.

Like any relationship regardless of the cultural influences, it was a testing phase, one we certainly needed, in order to clarify any false impressions…. much less obvious to read though, given the pretense defining the specific environment. We were on *his turf*, the codes heavily imbued in the manner of function, of communication, of dutiful observation to the given social order, of rigid structure.

There was little room for escape; this life choking with conformity…unlike the western ways; the individual focus, motivated by self-interest, desire to feed the ego…freeing up the spirit burning within, of creative inhibition.

As is customary for Japanese couples, and perhaps for most, regardless of nationality, sexual pursuits terminate prematurely.

Interest in the bedroom wanes for the ordinarily married. Social pressures, work commitments, familial obligations feed into any private time with your partner. As a reflection of our mad paced, crazily driven yearning for the next dollar, relationships and their display of affection are limited escapades for puberty, or 'the wives lunching.'

Being here long enough to attest, affairs do run rife with nary a word mentioned, general amnesia blanketing the cheating, whitewashing any trace of infidelity, social blinkering of the extramarital, acceptability as par for the course.

Women seldom have a choice, even today, to file for divorce at the whiff of the *other* woman. For the devoted mother has made that decision, to give up work, stay at home, and look after her children. Totally dependent on him, she is not at whim to criticize the nightly activities of her husband's flings. She is to turn a blind eye to the shenanigans persisting behind her back, for one day it is believed, he will return to her nest.

Neither did my partner nor I gesture further any interest sexually; the desire to be aroused. A hiatus persisting, this relationship had gone to seed very quickly in **that** domain. Each of us recognized, rather shamefully and without address, the marriage, for what it stood for, had faded. We slept in separate rooms, in separate beds, our priorities syncopated, striving to survive, to get ahead. We were buddies, and behaved so…guys hanging out together… a brother I never had. It was safe, we knew our boundaries, nothing more yearned for, nor desired…which, for me, I could endure, as my appetite had yet to be awakened.

Letter 8:

The forces of fortune favor us all equally. Whilst we may express ourselves differently, we are all entitled to heavenly help. That's why you are due to get so much of it today.

I read my horoscope everyday...it is not a religion but my curiosity with this one astrologer as he is very good, and quite precise with his readings...it gives me comfort and helps me in my day.

Today's reading is the quote above, and all I can think of is your presence in my life to date. You are that heavenly messenger from somewhere above...I know this to be true! You have opened my eyes and made me realize, life is to love, and be loved, not some time-bending round the clock routine of chasing money. We can all survive, though the variables change according to circumstance but life is more than survival. You have made me understand this fact, you have woken me to the notion that life is so precious, we cannot afford to let it slip past us...we must grasp life in our two hands and be grateful for its mercy and kindness.

You are the heavenly messenger who has revealed this to me...for I have been sitting in the cave minding my business and not caring about such discoveries...not caring or fearing such a situation...yet you have pried open my door of existence and said... come with me...

Who are you! I sit here overwhelmed in wonder ...how could this be possible? Some celestial force is beaming down on this bond we are forging...it feels good, and it feels right...I am going to defend and protect what is so valuable to me ...

You are that heavenly being, that angel, that knight whether you realize yourself or claim to be...this is how I see you...nothing greater than the highest force from above! In the routine of our ordinary lives you have shown a love so sublime, hope and joy...life is to live, live is to love, love is the supreme expression overcoming fear....and you are revealing this to from afar...I get it now...I understand...

Thank you for opening my eyes to this fact...I must have read about it somewhere or seen it in a movie but now I recognize it, and believe that IT is love...

ANT BEARING ITS BURDEN...

The bond fraying and old, unravelling in its deconstruction...naked and cold....

We, my partner and I, had, as sadly some marriages become, hit the rocks so to speak...what was once at least *civil* in the literal sense, as how ours had been consummated (a dictate blanketing the relationship upon reflection), for the most part agreeable, polite as expected in conservative cultures, and to some degree respectful...had turned to a hostile environment....a battle as it were, tempered, tired and testing.

Work was the culprit, there was no one to blame....Upholders of limiting responsibilities, both of us bore the burden of the menial overflowing, tipping the balance of life and work...and thus was brought home to the 'office.'

Endless evenings were spent barking down the phone, ah yes the voice of authority to his subordinates, directives yelled, orders repeated, all in what appeared a grave sense of urgency. It was loud, irritating and tense...not very conducive for an evening's retirement...even on a Sunday....what was I to make of this? What with the bravado? Definitely not a turn-on ...suffering from Napoleon complex I began to suspect...a man of small stature with a mighty roar....but why begs the question, why? I didn't understand this at all.

No doubt, he was straining to perform, meet those deadlines, prove his worth in the new environment. It was demanding....you could hear it, even as my Japanese is elementary, there was no *mis*interpretation of the tone, and manner....the pressure palpable.... Periodically he had faced such conditions before, as was his choice career-wise.

A capable employee, he held posts for no more than four years, this being more customary in the West rather than in Japan. A *challenger*: a *Japlish* expression bandied about nowadays meaning to confront the new, and offset convention. He had remarkable determination, a confidence lacking in most guys here for fear of upsetting consensus, a wild abandon in his quest to succeed.

Like oil off a duck's back, nothing fazed him...gossip certainly was quickly doused...unlike myself where the very nature of petty-minded gossipers undermining your persona, your character, your identity just to belittle and quash, wrought havoc in my head...

Nevertheless the soldier single-mindedly was made to endure...for the sake of health, life, and no less important love.

All energy had drained long ago...the wick truly extinguished even as far back as the moment of tying the knot. We had tested the waters so to speak, confirming compatibility long before taking the plunge. No fools rushing in were we.

Yet what options were there, more pertinently did I have? We were comfortable together, a platonic bond, the brother I never had. We had a connection, a set of codes contextualized, unspoken, telepathic, intuitive... by its very nature Japanese. Communication was implied, and emotions *not* expressed directly for fear of destabilizing the *wa* (and for the record, imbued with shame, of losing face...not being true to your identity; not holding responsibility for who you are, nor how you feel as an individual beyond the collective...where did honesty become so prized?)

And so the exchange became constrained, reduced to reporting the descriptive... 'What he said, what she did'...regular fodder for the gossip-mongers among them.

Conversation in its fundamental essence was lacking...opinions codified, consensus blinkering all perspective...I began to lose my voice and my vision.

Letter 9:

You confronted me with a proposition I have not given enough thought to yet...the notion of being a mother to your dearest daughter...contemplating this incredible undertaking I have to tread carefully in following your guidance.

Naturally as a father, the birth of your own child as conceived by your first love must be a significant event in anyone's life...I do not know this experience...but only sense the incredible joy it must be in becoming a father for the first time...

The role of mother to Deborah, I am not your former wife...those shoes are too great to fill.

What I can try to be is a loving member of this new unit...things will test my sensibility ...this is by far the most challenging to date... yet I want to prove to you that through the trials and tribulations, this is going to work...I will have time to dedicate myself to this new role... learning the ropes as we go along...some days steady some days rough... but allow me this rare opportunity of taking responsibility for another....I have never been given such a chance....

This is the beauty of life...which I have only come to realize in meeting you now...it is not about the earnings, not about the fame, not about the prestige,....it is about the love that exists when touched by that special someone...that person who carries that torch across the heavens, over the oceans...to unite and commit as one....

You have brought me to this stand still in my life...and I have willingly accepted my fate...believing this to be the right thing for us...It will push my boundaries beyond what I imagine...but this is the essence of living and sharing, learning and loving....please don't consider me selfish ...I am new at this...my love...show me the way...

...Being a mother is learning about strengths you didn't know you had, and dealing with fears you didn't know existed....

I have been searching for love in all the wrong places...then you come along...

How can this be possible? I had almost given up expecting or hoping that one day an ideal partner would cross my path, and, as you have done, sweep me off my feet. Do such fairy tale romances exist? I am beginning to sense that love certainly works in mysterious ways...

PRINCE CHARMING

That guy had come into my life earlier...of somewhat curious circumstances...I had just been on a summer break and was exploring the wonders of Roma, traipsing the well-trodden paths in Italy. This was not the first time evidently...

Although no stranger to this corner of the globe, it never ceased to instil a sense of awe, nor subdue my passion for the place. I recall being at the Spanish Steps; a famous landmark where many a visitor congregates for various reasons...one notably perhaps for recollecting scenes in *Roman Holiday* starring Audrey Hepburn and Gregory Peck.

The noon sun streaming down, heating up the polished cobbles underfoot, many a visitor rested in languor, mesmerized by the timeless view.

We had just dropped by an antiquated establishment, an institution among the connoisseurs, *Antico Caffe Greco* for an espresso, the budget barely covering the privilege. Mirrored and well-framed were images of a by-gone era….Men and women, with an air of *de bonheur de vivre: joy of life*, draped in their finery all visiting the *caffe* for the regular restorative came to mind...the likes of a distant time beyond the tech -age all pervasive in our very existence today. This was a period of sense and sensibility, of convivial conversation, of philosophical meanderings, of exchanges only lovers would whisper...the intimacy of the salon, in private quarters of the well heeled.

In a stupor perhaps over stimulated by what may have been the afternoon heat, the caffeine, but enveloped were we in this drunken state...impervious to any of *plebeian peccadilloes*, we had no care in the world...and were happy to be led by what had inspired rather than guided.

We had just left, and were ambling along the narrow lanes behind the towering terraced blocks with no care as to our bearings. Wandering the less congested by-ways taking photos of gateways …the beautiful arches, the ornate doorknobs…these court-ways to another world, I vividly recall hearing music, someone practising the piano. It had awoken me, had pried open a chapter of my life thought completely sealed. The music Beethoven's *Pathetique* C Minor Piano Sonata no. 8, the 2nd movement. How I had labored or rather tortured the piece when I was student preparing for my final exams. What I haven't forgotten even today is that movement…to suddenly and unexpectedly come upon it in my journeys struck a chord overwhelmingly…Arresting, I stopped and crouched down by the curb in wonder…higher powers from above had blessed me with this opportunity to play audience to this one piece…how was this even possible….I later learnt there exists a conservatorium Saint Cecilia; the patron of music. It could have been any composition, any composer, any period, yet on that day, at the time, I was made privy to such workings, convinced that yes, the angels above were influencing their powers over me.

What transpired upon my return was no short of a miracle. At my doorstep there befitting my sight stood *that* guy, the *cliched* tall (unusually so in these parts of the woods,) dark of Asian persuasion, and handsome in a Euro-chic kind of way.

Self-conscious but not shy, he entered my space, peering carefully around the given boundaries. Far from salubrious, any pretense soon dispelled. As was customary, we sat Japanese-style on the laminated floor, cushioned yes, but comfortable… questionable. And so the repartee began.

No theme left unturned, this guy had a sense of the other, aware of the machinations of the Western world, an understanding, even an appreciation of the differences existing in the two spheres. Exchanging ideas, exploring notions, this was our luxury we could afford to philosophize, challenging our predispositions, confronting our perspectives. The cerebral *pas de deux* we engaged, our steps so carefully observed for fear of treading on the other. This interlude; a moment of respite from the ordinary, and what had sadly become mundane, enraptured me, had drawn me to momentarily escape but for a fleeting few hours each week.

He would return regularly enough, schedule permitting, usually as a brunch session, a civil hour of the day. To be in the company of such a refined specimen of beauty and *not* feel infatuated was an understatement. How I longed to meet him next…the excitement like that of a schoolgirl…nervous and silly.

It was fun... the highlight of my week...learning about his world, that of negotiation, contracts and trade, the gentleman's realm so remote from my modest functions; of verbal conjugations, agreements and expression. Fascinating to no end, he would mesmerize me with measured aplomb any number of topics related to *his* world in what now seems quite ordinary and banal but at that time of great import, executive, major league.

Revelling in discussion resuscitated my wellbeing...renewing hope in what appeared a life heading into a rut...yes, *he* was a miracle indeed.

We were comfortable with each other, on the same wave length so to speak, and all the while I kept pinching myself so as to prevent my mind wandering in a direction beyond the agreed exchange. Entertaining thoughts of pushing such boundaries were not made possible for lack of confidence for one thing, and the fact this delicate balance should reserve pursuing any notion of a brief fling....it was not worth sacrificing...we had, after all, invested time and energy in forging this bond, of platonic sorts as it would appear...

We would continue in this manner; the sharing of ponderings and meanderings, this journey we took together in my room was satisfying enough, the cravings of the physical diminishing over time...but not completely extinguished.

A shift in priorities, of schedules clashing would force us to shelf the sessions. Periodically flashbacks of our exchanges would cross my mind...a memory of a past distancing over time. The girls may have flocked about this handsome specimen of a man, but I had been granted that insight so precious, of the intellect engaged, and how I held those moments dear to me for a period of time.

For an interval of few years, would we find ourselves reconnected. The wonders of the digital: social networking system SNS would grant us this chance to rekindle what little was remaining.

He had initiated the move. Lacking in tech know-how, a reflection of my generation perhaps, it wasn't until days later would I find the *messenger* had delivered. We had picked up from where we had left off; the banter light, the repartee convivial, I was spirited away, back to that familiar space, so cozy and inviting.

It was agreed to meet for dinner, we had never done this before...gone on a 'date' proper....How this simple proposal would play havoc with my emotions I cannot begin to describe....the volatility more aggressive than the stock market index after a collapse...indicative of the time.

The first date was, at the last minute, cancelled. I knew I was not prepared emotionally to face him, to hold an air of confidence without caching my true affections. He respectfully acknowledged my decision, and so another week would pass before I could muster enough courage to finally meet him. Was I any more prepared? I doubt it.

Throughout the day my mind was racing with anguish: what if..., what if..., what if... Upon meeting, naturally my heart was pounding, my mind swamped, blurring all thoughts, choking all feeling... I was on high alert. He sensed this state I was in, and reserved, as gentlemanly, any approach.

Sitting in the *Benz* only made me feel more detached from this world: his reality. 'You've made it!' The image of the three-pointed star... how I had come a long way girlfriend! Though such embellishments rarely impress, it was nevertheless a symbol of status...of having arrived.

Sitting at the counter of a busy upmarket *izakaya: Japanese bistro* (even for a Monday night!), food didn't entertain the course of events.

We were catching up...Absorbed in the interaction at play, my full attention was given to each and every word enunciated, the stories *truly* captivating, the ambience easing my tensions...and so I was reminded once again of how comfortable we had once been. The giddiness of the Catholic schoolgirl, how quaint she appeared, not quite shaken, he was observing, teasing, anticipating his next moves.

The lighthearted banter continued on the drive back to my apartment.... he was dropping me off, of course. We would toy with, and only subtly, undertones suggestive, lending to a gentle teasing, a foreplay of sorts, so to speak. And stealthily the boundaries had shifted, the demarcations lifted, the edges blurred...we found ourselves lost in an embrace... Not a haphazard brush on the lips, a peck on the cheeks, no, we were eager to explore this side never ventured. What had triggered that, I cannot comprehend, but it felt good, it felt right, and with little resistance, Pandora's box was tapped open.

Like any woman, lacking any attention of a sexual nature for an extensive period; for me it was well over ten years, even the slightest gesture had triggered an overly sensitive desire, of heightened arousal, sexual yearnings...

How do you think I responded to this dose of passion by none other than the one infatuated?

...the Prince Charming who, had made his presence in my life several years ago, had triggered in me a hunger for something greater, a lust for the forbidden fruit, a desperate need to be had. A drought for way too long, suddenly burst forth a *tsunami* of emotions flooding my soul.

My mind was screaming YES! This is what I want, this is what I crave, this is what would define me as a woman. And like a teenager with her first kiss all a trembling, I fell into the abyss of lust, confusing love for sexual awakening, and thus redefining our relationship as such.

Our next *rendez-vous* as it were, discrete, unassuming, we were to meet at the same spot as for dinner...this time a trip to Kyoto for the weekend.

Despite the cocktail of emotions: the agitation, the excitement, the anticipation, the fear, I would go bravely, appear the modern and sophisticated, a woman of the world! (A throwback to Sex and the City anyone?) And yet conflicts of guilt soon began to creep in. Ah Catholic guilt, the one and only, fashioned at birth, our DNA coding, the sin, oh the sin. And just like that we met, jumped on the next *shinkansen*: bullet express train, and we left.

Both of us realizing the impact of our decision on this relationship; he agreed, I was prepared.

A consensus of sorts unspoken...we were on our field trip of exploration, the surroundings limited to the boudoir, despite the attractions of the old capital. We embarked into the forbidden zone, one of lust and temptation.... of biblical proportions (for me anyway!)

Tasteful surroundings furnished our privacy, of modern Euro-chic...None of the reference to anything Japanese, we had entered this augmented reality you could say, dislocated by time and space. We could have been in any one of the capitals in the world, take your pick. The backdrop fitting for our quest.... let the fantasy begin...

Not so easily as it would appear though. A race of questions flooded my mind, only to seek reassurance, in a vain attempt to muster courage desperately required at this the eleventh hour: what is happening, is this real, what will happen next, will I meet expectations, will he be satisfied, what if I fail to perform, how do I measure up to the others he may have had before?

Churning over in my head these questions would hinder and block, to a point I could not make that distinction between what was pure chemical receptors, my emotions, my feelings...there was too much going on in my head.

As in the initiation of any sexual contact, the mating dance began...slowly and gently at first. How magical to the touch it was; behind the ears, on the neck, the nerve-endings charged, I was fully aroused and ready to surrender to the forces that be...We were to spend the next 48 hours in such a state.... the room was in complete disarray; the furnishings cleared for more space, the cushions tossed to one side, the covers tangled in a corner, the setting...a display of the wild escapades of this our new adventure. The disorder perhaps a mirror of my mind at that time....tossed, tangled, a total shamble.... But how wondrous this sensation ....how satisfying was 'it'....relief from the tensions bubbling within ...I needed more.

Letter 10:

How did you know to arrive in my life when all else was failing? The little affection I had once had for my 'partner' had been drained and under strain...and I had thought well, I must accept my lot...You come along and open my eyes, and wake me up to the reality that I have choices and can steer a future independent of my current situation.....for that I am deeply grateful.

The impact you have made is magnanimous...beyond my wildest imagination...a bearer of hope, a creator of dreams, a design of love... how can this have fallen in my arms?

You have stirred in me emotions I have only recently discovered...a depth so profound it makes it hard to breathe for fear of falling over (which I have already done on the train!) Yet the impact has been felt literally oceans away...all of this has been purely emotional, of the mental faculty and of the physical actually.

I have a picture in my mind of who you are ...an attractive guy with a charming smile...But it is the words, the gestures, the commitment, the dedication, the honor of your word that has impressed me the most...you are a genuine guy with true convictions...you mean what you say, and proceed to follow through.....I do not doubt you at all and it is this trust that has boosted my confidence in you.

Call me crazy but I have fallen deeply in love for you...and yet we hardly know each other...how can this be? The precious moments together, the exchange of messages, the simple gestures of commitment have made me realize...this is real. I have never met anyone with such integrity and dedication...so keen to fulfill his duties...as a man....ah my king!

My life will change in so many ways...I do not fear this...I welcome the challenge. Naturally Deborah, our daughter will take priority in the responsibility of care and dedication, which I am committed to upholding...this new chapter in all our lives; yours, Deborah's and mine will grow from strength to strength...the right amount of nurturing and love knows no limitations...investment here is for life...that is the commitment I am prepared to seal.

Where this will take us...I am only hope forever in blissful content.....I want to be one of those couples still holding hands at over 80...with a

glimmer in our eyes...and a smile so wide... we are and remain in love....
let that be us...

I want for you to feel complete with me...and am going to make every
effort to dedicate my life to you...this is no sacrifice... this is my gesture
of gratitude for coming into my life at a most critical time...

REAL ESCAPE GAME

Cracking the mystery of definition, Of how to fathom the lustful appetite of women.

A conquest of sorts, confounds even today researchers of the physiological, psychological, and quasi-logical. It cannot be pinpointed to one aspect, the rationale behind the infinite baffling. Failing to classify, to encode, we are left none the wiser in understanding womenfolk. She must be left to her own devices, to identify and capture that very essence of desire.

This craving unquenchable, of libido ravenous, this edged me to venture forth, be that pioneer, be bold, have the confidence to dare. I was plain of physique, healthy and fit, yet not sexy in the conventional way; no jugs for *tits*, no *arse* for riding, just ordinary so to speak. There was never a 'special drawer' for goodies to stimulate the activities in the boudoir, the marital suite. No lingerie, you know the kind, somewhat sexy, revealing in just the right places, of fine silk or lace; delicates never slutty and cheap. Nor were there attachments or equipment stimulating the drive to do it... There was never a need...That did not exist.

In the given climate, there was no interest in 'putting on the face,' pandering to social mores if you like....applying and powdering, of penciling and pouting, enhancing and concealing as most women do.

Even on the trains here in Tokyo, on the daily commute with a billion workers crammed up against each other you find held reflecting hand mirrors, mascara touching up the lashes, rouge applied liberally despite precariously positioned, totally absorbed in *her self,* of appearances, regardless of the less than conducive conditions, and with a stare aloof and vacant; a gal gotta do what a gal gotta do kind of attitude.

'Mary, Mary quite contrary, how does your garden grow?'

I was content in my own skin, and had grown out of the artifice of making up for the pretense.

What had triggered this yearning was quite obvious. I had had none for so long.

What compounded this drive stemmed from being deprived, rejected, and even discarded (or how I felt) for choice pickings at the 'salon d'affaires', the hostess bars, soaplands; local pseudonym for brothels, the bordellos, how else was I to react?

It has now become apparent in this land here, this notion of cheating on your spouse, in most cases, is often overlooked by their wives. Subjugating fully to the needs of their husbands, rarely is the topic of infidelity breached in their home environment. The lore of the land: It benefits the women not to flinch when it comes to the roving eye of their husbands despite the consummation of marriage.

The common adage only revealed to me recently is held by many yet admitted by few, the view that a marriage be a woman's grave for all the hardships, burden, and sacrifices made. When in the equation a mistress appears, her life of misfortune is profoundly instilled.

For it is said that the urges of men may not be adequately met in the matrimonial suite.

E voila, the existence of *soaplands* and the like, are a wonderful option for the sexual urges unsatisfied. Local logic being; so long as the emotional component does not intervene, justifies the acceptance, a distinct separation indeed! And thus their cheating partners are given the green light. What privilege to be granted, approved by their own women, their wives, to philander under the guise of blowing off steam.

Determined to prove myself sexually attractive, even desirable, I needed to vanquish the 'husband', to take revenge. And so this mission began. This mighty surge of hysteria pierced my heart, tarnished my soul, destabilizing me beyond approach: don't mess with me, a woman scorned.

General consensus would proclaim testosterone enables men smooth sailing somewhat unaffected emotionally when compared with women. The chemicals released as physiologically attested, act as a buffering effect against mood swings, stress and depressive states in the broader sense.

For the man he is wired quite simply it is agreed; to gratify his sudden impulses, perhaps triggered by a drunken night out with the lads, cheating may indeed occur to satisfy the physical, of getting laid for the fun of it.

Symptomatic of estrogen levels in women, on the other hand, swings of balance on the sensitivity scale are identified; their tendency to retire early due to exhaustion, anxiety, stress; these daily pressures of life play into how reality is met. If, for instance, the spark has all but dissipated...of the semblance of love dissolved, smoldering can take place, brooding and the like, invariably leading to a loss of sexual appetite, and, in turn, complete closure on that commitment. For it is said she has emotionally checked out, this current relationship unfulfilling, seeking another conquest elsewhere to be had.

Hot-headed, on a rampage, dying for more, this wild wanton woman demanded to be fed. To revel in my quest, pursue this passion of revenge... alas to no avail my satisfaction would be met.... The guy was preoccupied with responsibilities of the office and, like most Japanese compelled to refrain from outside interests even of the more diluted variety; like a hobby, play time with the kids, I was sadly left...shrouded in frustration: beset by a desperate state of confusion...Taking action: a dent in this our arrangement called a 'marriage' was my quest ...but how?

Then he came along...

CURIOSITY KILLED THE CAT, OR DID IT?

As it would happen, he popped into my life unexpected. As if a messenger from above had been tuning into my every thought, secretly extracting the codes of desire, hacking into my personal files on emotions and all matters of the heart.

It was nothing I had imagined; he literally appeared on my smartphone screen, a circular framed profile of an individual unfamiliar. Who was he? How had he accessed my address? Had *I* contacted him before? Questions of the ilk started playing with my head...I was curious to know how he eased rather brazenly into my life, and quite charmingly made his presence hence, imposing on my personal space.

Previous to the initial contact, in my search for industry-based peers, I had sent out messages as a measure, perhaps desperate, to catch up on the threads of business unfamiliar. I had just launched a web site catering to the luxury-end diners visiting Japan. Recognising a *real* need for such a service in a world insular and unaccommodating to the particulars of a voracious tourism surge, I was confident such insight would carry me despite my inexperience. Linking up with fellow peers through SNS enabled me to get connected, and with little reservation, I embarked on this mission to get acquainted.

Up to this point, it was an attempt in earnest to learn from others, share in the exchange of ideas, and benefit from the relationships forging...a straightforward and positively healthy approach to using the tools at hand. Never was there a hint of the malevolent; no hidden agendas, no manipulation, nor pressures of business deals real or imagined. We were as it were a community, of sincerity genuine, of support trustworthy. So naturally in such a realm, confidence in corresponding with others grew. I was relating to people beyond these shores, on a global platform, I was becoming a member of this community, and for the first time ever I was connecting to people of my own.

Then he came along...and how did we meet again? To this day I am baffled. As to the source of this connection...I have no idea. An oddity, a curiosity, naturally I was seduced by this mystery. And just like that, a bonding of sorts emerged. A friendly few words of exchange, a joke, light banter, this was a soothing reminder of how *nice* people were in the world, or so it would appear.

This friendship extended gave me solace, as I had been distracted by issues on the home front. A recent unearthing of incidents had triggered a world wind blow to my stability; the discovery of the husband's extra-marital liaisons, his frequenting of whore houses and the like had stunned me speechless. And you know, I did not have to look hard for the evidence either! It was literally right in front of me.

Strewn at my feet, among the bundle of laundry and sundries in the corner there lay the evidence. Scattered on the floor of the spare room cum walk-in wardrobe were the *meishi:* business cards of a number of industry-related joints. Professionally embossed, at first I mistook them for standard commercial enterprises, and not of the 'after 5 p.m.' variety, mind you. Given the fact my Japanese language skills are rudimentary at best, I had ignored investigating such details, as it would seem, for a very long time. It wasn't only the business cards. On further inspection, in the chest of drawers (oh the irony here!) were found copious receipts stuffed, addresses written on the back of coasters, love letters just shoved in a pile...in total a collection well over fifty were found, right there, right under my *bleeding* nose. Evidently no attempt was made to conceal the proof, he assuming I wouldn't be able to read or comprehend the information...how brutish!

Some may beg the question why didn't you notice this before? Never had I entertained such thoughts. Why had there been a need to do so, was my attitude. How naïve was I!

Never had it crossed my mind that affairs, his *rendez-vous*, his frequenting of *bordellos*, that prostitutes existed, and sadly it had been going on for some time. Never had it been suspected, never had I thought it apparent in our marriage... I had no idea.

Dysfunctional marriages draw inquisitive minds to your predicament, certainly frowned upon in the public sphere. To lose face, oh the shame! To be covered, and smothered in cultural refrain, the evidence well hidden from scrutiny...imagine the prized fodder for the gossipers here. To quash all such matters is preferred, that being acceptable procedure.

Though enacted locally, the legal decree indoctrinated since Henry the Eighth's ruling, sadly to the unenlightened rarely is petitioned. Confronting the circumstances before us in the Western paradigm, an affair would be handled by the family court in due time. Despite the paramours that exist behind the hidden screens, very few would admit to divorcing, and taking custody of the kids.

At this discovery, my head was racing overtime, attempting to piece together any recollection of his playing the field, scratching my brain for any ounce of circumstantial evidence. I could recall none. I was mad crazy, desperate to right a wrong, and in vain, seek to take revenge.

Who was this sex-crazed monster I had married? As was revealed, the evidence collected dating back to a time when we had agreed to *tie the knot*. Perhaps this expression does not translate here, well certainly not in his mind anyway, for that commitment was not sealed....perhaps knotted with issues not yet realized.

What amazed me the most was the frequency of such visits; and the letters of gratitude as only the Japanese do with sheer finesse. 'Dear loyal patron...it was great to have you visit...we are hoping to see you soon...' Hand written, in the feminine cursive *hiragana,* saccharine dripping from the two page invitation, invariably cheap pink paper no doubt bought at the 100- yen store. An occasional lipstick mark stained the back side (another double entendre, oops!)

What had triggered this, I am beyond words. I suspect it may have to do with the fact that, once again, being on his turf, and meddling with his own: 'Japanese working women,' he felt entitled to do so as is customary for many a *salary* man married or otherwise.

What disturbed me the most was the amount of time, and money spent on such endeavors. This had surely been indicative of our incompatibility on all fronts: physically, mentally and emotionally insolvent. No attempt was made to join forces, perhaps out of fear or shame I surmise, neither of us desiring to address the issues of meeting satisfaction, we were as it seems, essentially functioning under the same roof merely getting ahead for the sake of survival.

And there lay the crux of the matter…this contract should never have been accepted…we were two beings with completely different perspectives on what constituted marriage.

For him, he could skirt issues extra-marital by conveniently frequenting locales unfamiliar to me. He could hide, and go about his business; the quest for blowing off steam, for seeking immediate gratification…indulging in the lascivious.

Born at the end of the 60s, even in my somewhat liberal ways, experimenting with *sex, drugs, and rock n' roll* reflective of my generation pre-digital, I was open to the less conventional, accepting of the choices of my generation, rarely criticizing lifestyles. That was my disposition, border-line hippy I guess, but it was my way of getting along in the world.

How should I have reacted? I did indeed panic…despite the liberal bohemian twenties.

I was inherently conservative with views of marriage. Far from sheltered, my formative years were exposed to the offbeat, nonconformist attitudes. I was privy to the depth and breadth of life's idiosyncrasies having left home on my 20th birthday, and needing to fend for myself independent of my parents.

Life's tableaux was the canvas of inspiration to broaden my horizons, to explore the wonders of the universe, shaping a certain perspective on the world.

It wasn't as if laissez-faire attitudes to the institution of marriage were unfamiliar. Mass media accounted for that. As it generally does, such platforms of communication penetrate our every waking hour, for good or bad depending on your view, exposing and imposing an augmented reality beyond our own.

In all honesty, my interpretation of what a marriage meant lay in the foundations of an altogether conservative bent. You marry for love, endeavoring to uphold such principles of trust and respect, and no matter what challenges, support each other preserving this, a sacred bond. Simply put, much harder to maintain, yet the tenets remain, one would hope, universal.

An interesting fact has dawned on me recently, when in ancient Roman times, it was the woman's privilege governed by law, to fully control their menfolk from wandering beyond the sacred chamber, the matrimonial bed, their love nest. For it was scribed, any ejaculation during intercourse be solely made in the body of his bride, his wife, his partner for life. To recognize this in court was to insist, the role of the betrothed was to receive sperm for procreation…and that was it!

Yet upon my discovery, this very fact left me in a stupor beyond recognition; the emotional barometer fluctuating incessantly, the rage burning within, only egging me further into a flurried state of despair. I had become a desperate woman, lacking any sense of identity in the role of this relationship, a woman robbed of her dignity.

A woman whose self-worth had plummeted, no less dramatic than the *Lehman Shock,* and emotionally terrified, took measures into her own hands, none other than to pursue divorce.

Incidentally I have you know, a code was devised to govern the issues of adulterous behavior; The Napoleonic Code Article 324, enacted not that long ago in 1810, all concurring in the courts of old, had a rippling effect in the minds of men all bouffant and robed.

For it was deemed intractable the lot of a woman, to contemplate being unfaithful to her husband. The *frail of sexes* falling to temptation, oh the public castigation, nothing less than the death penalty held for a woman and her lover at the will of the husband. And what of the flip side, I hear you ask, not a *soupcon* be mentioned for the unfaithful husband. Easily overlooked, and without debate, the women fell victim to the system misogynistic... A real piece of cake!

Letter 11:

Your connection with me has made me realize...there is goodness in this world...people are kind, and loving, and peace can be restored...I love that you, the torch bearer of light, of hope, of joy have sailed the oceans, swept the heavens and are prepared to carry me with you to a bright future... the unknown....

I do not fear this precipice that stands before us...I feel confident the steps we take together are the right ones...this is our destiny...it was written in the stars and guided you here to me...I do not fear this because love has convinced me this is right...you have proven this already...I do not fear our relationship as I am investing all that I have in the belief love is our foundation...

You are to become my man...and I your woman...

Who is the man I hardly know?

I asked this question when we first started our exchange....naturally I was curious ...at the same time impressed by the fact you would say such things to me...

As time passed, you revealed your personality...you can be quite funny! As well as your softer side....I have been learning who it is making such an impact ....

Though we haven't even sat face to face yet (I cannot wait for that day!) my mind has an impression of what makes you the charming, considerate, dedicated, committed not to mention lovable guy I have ever known....that is set in my memory due to the effort made, the words expressed, you being there each and every time....

How do I deserve someone like you in my life?

DAMSEL IN DISTRESS

Fuming with anger, a rage so livid, wildly seething below the still collected facade for keeping up appearances, I pursued this quest to avenge. Intractable, it was as if in a deluge of despair, I was neither logical, nor objective, nor rational. I was embroiled in a mesh of emotional aberration, clearly going hysterical.

Seeking the support of a counsellor was never an option considered as I was not aware of such a system accommodating dare I say in English, given the environment. Why would there be a service; the amount of huddling, conspiring and gossiping that goes on.... The existing networks all naturally serve to harbor against, as a buffer, any anomalies in this world. I did not belong...nor did I have the benefit of, such a sisterhood.

This society of women is an interesting bunch. Broadly speaking they are broken down into four categories; the *Careerists* all ambitious, ready to tackle the male dominance. The sweet petite *Princesses* all groomed and prim; capturing the heart throbs of their Disney-fed princes. In contrast we see the *Desperate housewives*, a clique of sorts whiling away the hours sipping café lattes and worrying about their nails. Not to mention the *Bad Girls*, with that tough exterior, an attitude fostered by the subordination to a gang-like association. The first three types more favorably hunt for their husbands -to -be. The goal in life, it seems for the majority, is to settle down and breed a family. How quaint to uphold such traditional roles, a woman's lot unchanged since the year dot.

There was one person I turned to for recourse; the character I believed I could trust, confide in, who fell under the guise of not only a student, but also a friend. The boundaries had blurred ever since our initial schedule. We were of similar age; yet socially divided. She had firm foundations already rooted within a system that served her well.

Being an audience of one, with myself an outsider, a foreigner enabled her to spout freely, at whim, any views unrestricted, free from the social mores of her culture, for that brief moment of escape. As for me, it was in fact a healthy reprise from the standard drone often produced.

Ever since I can remember she was inquisitive of Western ways, especially of the *boudoir* nature. *Sex and the City* the HBO TV drama from the US, was now, after 5 years of launching globally, finally approved by the body of purveyors; those upholding the revered principles of society. For what reasons it took such time, I cannot explain. At least it was given the thumbs up and broadcast nationally. It was better late than never I suppose. I had been watching most of the series through rentals…there is always a way of getting around the 'official' delays.

She had memorized each character's name, habit, and current status. This was her moment of indulgence…her afternoons a lotus-eater…and so we would discuss at length all facets of sexuality within 'proper' context, sufficient for an intermediate-levelled comprehension. Traces of sybaritic delight surfaced, genuine curiosity detected. Not overly versed in such matters, and cautious of not confusing roles and responsibilities, we carried on under the guise of 'learning English' for a period well over five years. Hence my sense of confidence in seeking her advice, regarded as a kind of mentor, a peer, a mate.

In hindsight I should never have resorted to her aid. I had turned to the wrong person; yet she was the only one I could confide in, when it came to such matters, or so I believed.

That one person I divulged my frustrations domestic was in fact a divorcee herself; only giving a year for it, the marriage, to terminate.

How the drama unfurling had piqued her inquisitive nature. Just like a character from her favorite drama, she was *dying* to know more. When we would meet, which seemed more frequent, either for the fact she wanted to feed off the episodes of my struggle, or she simply had more time, I am doubtful of the latter; it gave her wicked delight me recounting my fiendish matter.

Curling derisively at the corner of her mouth was wry bemusement, symptomatic of a brooding spinster or so it seemed.

Do it, why of course!

There was never any doubt in *her* mind that this be the route to take. No attempt to prevent my wallowing in grief, averting the problem, never an alternative solution be on the offer. Her encouragement in my pursuit only served to entertain her rather ordinary 9- to- 5 routine.

And what juicy morsels of fodder came to light for the gossip -mongers among her own. Yes, the rumors, how enticing….for most seeking an escape from their rather ordinary lifestyle. 'Feed me more, so that I may be entertained,' perhaps even believing every word of it.

Nasty pieces of work those who instigate, carried by sneerers, spread by the idiots, and without surprise accepted by the majority of ignorant fools among them.

It was better than any soap opera watched, she claimed… as the drama intensified on the home front, so too did the beguiling nature of her intrigue. She reveled in the thickening plot, no doubt a topic of 'particular' fascination around a few bottles of red, or white at the local *izakaya*: pub among her friends, colleagues and family. All the while, in my hysteria, complete profusion of the heart, a draining of the soul, I was left vulnerable, emotionally destitute.

Dearest fraulein,

'Twas it you who made me stumble…in my madness, without grace you watched from afar, the dismay. Was it schadenfreude, me keeping you entertained, a bemusement at my expense? Your petty little mindedness, clearly lacking substance, leaves me wondering how this so called friendship ended up a mess.

There was no comfort, no shoulder to cry, none of which was apparent… it was not quite like that of the t.v. dramas I watched. She was there alright, listening to my every word, tolerant of my outbursts all the while relishing in my frustrations…yet the support would not be found…or rather it was obscure beyond recognition…especially in my state of mind…imperceptible on all levels.

None the wiser, I stuck to my guns, to pursue my quest in making him suffer…Looking back at that time, was I also quietly satisfying her expectations, was I pleasing her? The old adage misery likes company never rang so true.

Letter 12:

Crossing oceans of sea, sometimes pretty high from my understanding, you are willing to come to greet me...I have never heard of such commitment...this fact alone has knocked me over completely...who is this man? I keep asking myself.

You express your love so openly with me...I have known no other...and love it when you say those three words.... I become unsteady sometimes... and need to sit down.... That is the impact you have made....

Over the course of exchanges we have grown in our company...and as a consequence...so has our love for each other...I believe it to be equally powerful...I want you in my arms....you are there....but oh, the day we meet what fun we will have... exploring each other for the first time...like some teenages...your embrace is warm....I can feel that now...and can only imagine how you smell...a turn on already!

We live for that day when we can finally solidify our love....this is real, and you and I are one...the same...forever amen...

To be blessed in knowing such a man, I cannot explain....this thing of beauty you have possessed me, consumed my every waking day and sleeping night, who causes me to stir so strongly on hearing I love you....I must hold in my two arms...and cherish for an eternity.

I offer you my love, my life, my soul to you, the man who loves me.... hoping to fulfill your expectations...I dedicate myself fully to you...I want to complete you, complement you, be your counter-balance in love, and in life.

You are what is the most important to me right now...I am determined to uphold that promise...naturally Deborah plays an equally top priority as our daughter...but you as my lover, my life partner, my husband and king, this is my commitment to you....to love and to hold forever....

You have displayed a generous outpouring of love for me...I have never known....but how I love it so...you have embraced me...how warm that feels....I want to stay here with you forever...

FAR FROM THE MADDENING CROWD

Are we wired to be monogamous?

This devotion to your one and only, may befit a fairy-tale existence but we are *mere* mortals naturally induced by our environment. Why then the constant resistance to temptation, even if unrelenting?

Crises averted?

By keeping to the straight and narrow undoubtedly blinkering our vision.... Should we ignore our fundamental instincts, perhaps basal for some lofty ideals ethical and principled....for what purpose? To suffer in denying what could be possible? Is it therefore *not* our destiny to attain happiness in love, in life? And what if, at first, *Eros* fails to hit that target, are we doomed to endure, a prison sentence if you will, and bear this burden to death do us part?

Life, a celebration of love, should be shared and enjoyed, not to be captured, bottled, and corked as a genie lamp to be occasionally rubbed, (imagine if you will) but free to express, relish and savour.

How much happier our world would be without such precepts corseting and binding our natural urges...

In a series of months, my life would transform. Swinging from limb to limb, my arms overly extended and aching, I would clutch onto those branches for dear life, for fear of plummeting into this pit of desolation. The *prince* had parted ways, the husband divorced, I was deflated, rejected, and scorned.

In the midst of all this commotion, there he was.....my pop-up character... offering his gesture of friendship. And so I, in my apparent state, welcomed this apparition and responded.

Innocent at first, my impressions were nothing but positive...a welcoming reprise to the tensions boiling over. A repartee of sorts soon developed, every

Sunday afternoon he would appear; I soon began to expect him there before high tea. We grew suddenly, bonding ever so intimately, I felt I knew this guy.

The charm was nothing less than alluring. It was genuine delight, here was *a man I hardly knew* taking an interest in my affairs, my future, my life. Not one to initiate, (of course!) it was he who would make such contact, query my mind, affording me all this attention I had sorely wanted. And naturally I was enticed.

This zone of ours, how soothing it felt, how comforting; this was my escape. It was the balm to my grief and pain. I was at ease, a sense of calm embracing, there was hope in the world...I truly believed this *messenger* was indeed a godsend, an angel from above, the holy ghost!

As the frequency of his visitations increased, so too did my longing for him.

Measuring the degree of emotional intensity could be plotted to rationalise the propensity. Processing the power of his words, his expressions of affection, what I believed to be *love*, could be encapsulated in *Moore's law*: that which defines the correlation of variables as a fundamental constant.

A roadmap of sorts, the growth rates doubling in time...shaping a future unimaginable.

This parallel existence, proportional in behaviour, as reflective of the other, mimicking each other's motivation, not of causation it is determined. The consequence? Is there any limitation to this co-dependency, exponentially speaking?

If, to extrapolate on the *digital speak*, the surge of positive activity is not based on singularities, so let us imagine a binary system of variables: myself and the other....however you want to label him or her; a partner, a lover or a friend. With increasing connectivity, enhancing the experience, we give definition and add meaning to the paradigm transforming, fortifying and solidifying the relationship forming. In metaphoric context, a future unknown, we surrender to the forces unbridled, uncontrollable, merging of minds shifting favorably, possessed by a symbiosis entwining.

It is a well-known analogy presented to French children at an early age, of the need to recognise such mechanics at play. The simple water lily sitting on the surface of the pond, has the nature to double in its rate of growth, and so expanding its coverage on a daily basis. Insignificant at first, very little attention be given, until the swelling of plant life starts exceeding. It is proposed that in a period of a month, how soon would the strangling of life take heed? It is on the 29th day, at the final hour, that action be taken to circumvent the complete choking of nature, and save the pond.

This analogy proposed capitalizes on the fundamentals of mankind. Fraught with anxiety, new to any relationship the interaction of two variables, let's say a couple, is constantly testing boundaries undecipherable; when does it become overly tricky to pursue, where is the zone safe, what lines are drawn limiting how we feel, who decides what is correct and proper? Heavily codified, intellectualized, (and sadly somewhat mortified!) have we lost all recognition of man's existence, his modus operandi for life, if you will.

The *transhumanist* thinkers study the potential benefits and dangers of emerging technologies that, as quoted, 'could overcome fundamental human limitations,' of man's struggle, ethically speaking, in forging a working relationship beyond the mechanics of robotics. Let us suppose for a moment that instead of the interaction between man and sophisticated gadgetry, we step back and look more closely at the essence of human connection, and how greatly this, itself, can enhance the intellectual, physical and psychological capacities.

What about in love? Are we not positively transformed, the playful synergy at work, counterweighing the shifting balance, supporting and sustaining the equilibrium present. Is that not man's reason for a partnership, to share in the beauty of life together; nurturing the growth, guiding the forces, fusing the elements, welding a power so strong to overcome the intrinsic limitations of the individual self? Perhaps blindingly so, convinced that *he* is the one....that this is so.

To recognize and adapt,
Be sensitive to the constants,
Accommodate for the variables,
And monitor the swings of nature; the bedrock of sustainability.

And thus, in this quest for unravelling the mystery of love in our lives, is all this in vain? I beg to differ...

Letter 13:

My dearest and sweetest man I have ever known Wesley, keep safe in the knowledge you will weather this trouble, overcome this challenge and meet me at the end.

Consider me as that northern star in the night sky, guiding you, keeping you clear from the dangers that lurk ....I want you to believe that with my help, you will pull through to safety.

This is a challenge for both of us; you facing the imminent threat I can only imagine....and me worrying about your predicament. But we can and will endure...this is the final test we must face before we can seek a freedom of our life together.

I am your northern star....for I rest here and shining down on you each and every minute....this light I am radiating is now switched to full... and when you look up...it is I who is there looking over you, ensuring your protection....

Undivided is my focus, I will lead you here to a secure place where you find comfort and joy...and love....Pay attention to what's around you...move cautiously, stealthily but move forward...I am your magnet drawing you away from the present dangers encroaching. Will you do that for me...recognize the fact that with my love, this will sustain you, keep you from slipping, from running off course.

Believe in the fact you can trust me....your recent commitment displays this...I will do you no harm as I am prepared to devote my love, my life, my all to man I have only just met...do you know why?

You have demonstrated to me this unbridled devotion, this outpouring of emotion, this love on a level far beyond the stars in the night sky... no man in the world has ever attempted to extend himself in the manner that you have shown me...

SIMULACRUM

When played right, the physical awakening the spirit, reverberating within....
How does one put into words the wonders of nature stimulated, of ecstasy,
of climaxing reached, when transported beyond the ordinary to this place of
momentary bliss...the female orgasm...ah, the mystique.

To his instrument the virtuoso would play, plucking at the heart strings
ever so gently, sympathetic to the ear, naturally I gave sway.

With his bow legato would the tone be set, a gentle modulation, a lilting
progression.

A melody of singular nature, thematic coloration he would begin ever so
delicate, rising and falling notes held in full strokes, arresting my focus, passion
visceral resonating. As in Beethoven's *Pathetique* C Minor Piano Sonata no. 8,
the first movement *Grave* with its gentle subtlety, emerging and taking flight
variations transforming, to a state of spiritual unrest, of foreboding dissonance.
As was this subliminal relationship unfurling.

Unorthodox mode mixtures; the sharps and flats undulating in irregular
phrasing, reflective of the tone of sentiment, the degree of passion, the spirit
of mood.

Suspense lingering, Incessant apprehension insinuating, Emotional tension
captivated. As with any movement of greater complexity, Polyphonic interplay;
of motifs recurrent, A rondo of rich diversity arresting the spirit.

In lyrical grace the themes would glide, rhapsodic interludes of crescendo
would rise, of great intensity, drama and tempo, so too did the exchanges, our
intimate longings.

Of similar transition, the interaction was a beautifully harmonized
composition.

I fell mesmerized under this spell...Tearing at the very fiber of my being, I would shudder unnerved. How could *this man I hardly know* move me in ways yet realized.

As if in a hypnotic trance, I had succumbed to this enchantment enveloping. Stupendous, I surrendered to the forces at play, rendering me bewildered, lost for words. And yes, foolishly convinced myself... this was Cupid's doing.

In hindsight, had I all along simply needed that attention, to be loved?

The desire to be held, to be touched, to be had, for too long was lacking. This pining for attention not only of the emotional, but that of the physical became the strands draping my perception, my window on this world. Perhaps out of boredom, of lacking the comfort of a partner, the romance of a lover; there the rationale of behavior sprang forth, to bond with another, to quench the thirst of passion, of unleashing the repressed libido.

How was I to discern lust for love?

This emotional tsunami crashing at every break, would confuse my spirit and temper my nerves. The symptoms were there, as prescribed: High levels of dopamine associated with norepinephrine, heightening attention, short-term memory, hyperactivity, sleeplessness and goal-oriented behavior.... In other words, my focus remained intently on this exchange, albeit of the penned variety, and often on little else.

Given the emotionally shifted disposition, this stimulation only fed into my voracious hunger.

And just like food, tantalizing morsels tempted my palate, the appetite ravenous, never fully satiated. Indulgences, I had never known, perhaps reflective of my regular eating habits of old. Controlled, measured doses of nutrition sufficient for my daily needs, this had forever been my approach to consumption. This craving of the other, of desire, had only been awakened in the last few months...how the embers of passion enlightened glowed more intensely once heightened.

His presence was my nourishment, and how desperate I was for feasting whole...and there lay my weakness, I was becoming addicted, yes give me more.

Chocolate could, to a degree, momentarily take the edge off my tormented state...Yet the pervasive magnetism bewitching, passions wildly singeing my every nerve, I would not settle for a block of it, chocolate....I needed my hit, *Eros* shot from above...a moment to behold.

Levels immeasurable, this flooding of the hormone oxytocin, intoxicating the physical, pulsating my every nerve, overflowing the arterials, flooding my head; love in the physical sense.

How had he cornered me like no other, had preyed on my sensibilities, and coerced me into thinking that *he* was the one. Given all I had confronted, my vulnerability at its most raw, how I had fallen for the sentiment manifested; this, I was convinced, was a gift from heaven...and with such delight I indulged...quite uncharacteristic of who I had been, always goaded and prodded, guarded and protected, measured and dosed...how I relished in the realm of love unknown...Pure bliss indeed...this was furthest from any crazy dream imagined, there was no other, ...Unleashing the lust all inflamed, I was intoxicated...

Every night he would enter,
Play me slowly
Make me whisper...sweet nothingness
I would part my emotions, my feelings, my love,
How, I wonder in my lonely state, could such words be expressed so,
Why were they concealing, how much were they revealing,
Who would have known the poetry of love existing...

Letter 14:

I am affected by this magnetic pull you have over me...you have drawn me in...and as I am doing this now with you from the north... I need to reciprocate this same energy and drive to convince you that all will be fine...this is my first lesson from you...never give up on trying to pursue what you love...we are only here momentarily...life is too short...we must savor each and every moment as if it is our last...and run like crazy with wild ambition in the hope of attaining bliss....

You and I are now running toward each other... the path is well-lit.... the light beaming from both our souls brightening up this sometimes cold and dark world...we can identify each other in the darkness...no distance is too far...and as we move forward toward each other, the light only pulsates more radiantly, intensely burning to a point we can now feel that heat....we are almost there...no obstacle will block this path.... we have the faith and conviction we can make it....I believe in you, trust in you, and most importantly keep loving you unconditionally for an eternity... this is my pledge to you.

I am your northern star Wesley, know that is I guiding you to refuge...I am your beacon of light and strength ...reach out to me...hold me... for I won't let you go... you are moving closer to a secure spot...not far to go...you just need to push through this last passage before we can meet....

I am with you always...

PUPPETS ON A STRING

Discriminating minds are bi-polar delineated; of transcendence the fissured chasm.

This grey zone if imagined, with its infinite shades, is more convoluting to fathom; indistinguishable and hardest to claim. Oblique, obscure, and oftentimes overlooked, intrepid some venture forth, contemplating the variables, how wondrous their thoughts. Either foolish or genius, I guess it depends on influence. To curtail any perplexity, confusion and lose, parameters are set, the boundaries determined, alas the majority exist on the straight and narrow.

What tangled webs we weave...quick grab those secateurs, severe those ties ...release the bindings, relief and sigh.

Out of circumstance, perhaps reflective of mind, of environment, we find ourselves interconnected, enmeshed in thought, intertwined. We engage willingly, believing that humanity is essentially trusting, until proven otherwise. At what time does this frame of an individual be dissolved? At what limit do we lay to waste a relationship forging, turn our hearts against the wondrous spirit of mankind, shut down, switch off and discard the emotional tap guiding faith.

Self- preservation is the factor determining our gauge of response. Deflecting harm of the physical, mental and spiritual, these threats must be siphoned off...yet harder to detect some would say. Sentiment expressed, real or imagined, affects perception, and leads us into thinking that all is safe and sound.

Sadly things are misleading; when in fact it is a con artist devising a stratagem, deceptively menacing. Despite such foreboding, we deny the obvious, out of shame I guess, and accept that this is the predicament... How foolish are we, to assume such a position? Or can we test the factors influencing, at the same time fending off the wrenching of our vulnerability?

How can we be blinded by forces unforeseen? The solution: Imposing barriers and severing ties completely…is that the only way of existing?

Indulging the emotional traction at play, is this a dangerous notion to be kept at bay? What delineates our response to situations clouded in mystery…blind faith that God does provide, support and be here at the eleventh hour willingly?

How does one reverse the workings of the mental inflicted by which the spiritually sabotaged is lingering? Switching from incapacitation and paralysis to that constructive and healing, the shifting from the dark to the light, takes courage, conviction, an honesty confronting the skeletons hidden…

Lost in this labyrinth the mind struggles for answers. The most afflicted of all is that of sensibilities. Of the physical, miraculously over time, endurance persists and survival though stifled, stabilizes. The emotional battle is more complex, forces drugging the ego, squashing the id, suffocating the self through regular servings imbibed. 'What he wants, what I need…' the tug of war at battle, when will this cease?

Enmeshed in these complexities, we learn to surf the waves enraging. Requiring a tough core, only a person of substance resists this tsunami of tension engulfing. At every turn choking, struggling to breathe, triggering this desperation to survive, to fight back, and contradict. Which course to adopt, what direction to take, the choices though apparent, fail to prevail, and so we break down in fright and panic…how does one persevere?

Reality takes on a whole different perspective, one charged with feelings conflicting. Bound by the irrational, the illogical, what triggers such agitation plaguing the barometer; that measuring the ordered and sensible, of what is right and proper. Borne out of frustration, we assume a position justifiable.

How would the Bastion of Standards and Compliancy set parameters curtailing such matters distressing?

The path of the long and narrow seems the perfect fit, but what of emotional sustenance? Psychological stability, physical satisfaction, to deny them are we but playing at fashion? Like pieces on a board, the movement is swayed, designated by the doppelgangers far away.

If we are to step outside the rigidity of such boundaries, do we not expose ourselves to life's magical mysteries? Should we not take heed, and venture forth into the unknown… a certain quest of sorts.

What we will discover is yet to be revealed, by not pursuing this notion, have we failed to really live?

Letter 15:

Is this real?

I often question whether the circumstances unravelling before me are a fiction, t.v. soap, a drama. Part-action, part-suspense, but mostly romantic...I often wonder is this real?

I have come to accept that in the time we have known each other, I have grown to trust the man I now call my husband. You have proven time and time again your commitment, your honor and your integrity for which I am truly in wonder. Very few have the fortitude, the strength of character that you have displayed in the concentrated time together.

How this life pans out nobody knows....but I have faith that the love of my life will guide me in the direction, will be there for me as he is now, and will love me as he does. Those simple words 'I love you' constantly remind me that the man I love feels the same way as I do, and has no fear of stating that fact.

The individuals that make up this stage of life have helped to build and strengthen my conviction that this is no fairy tale...this is real. Deborah, our daughter, a beam of light, is at the center of this bond we have. She needs to be loved, to be guided, and as a role model be supported...and yes, she is real! Your contact Mr. Alex Odudu, though I have not met, has been consistent in his correspondence, confirming and gracious for the support received.

And then there is you Wesley...my love, my husband, my all. My life has made a 360' degree turn and is spinning at such a great pace... sometime s I need to sit down and take a breather. The impact you have, is life changing... I have been so mesmerized by you, that now at this junction in life, I have chosen to follow. I want to because I believe in you, and realise that what we share goes far beyond what words can express... it is a deep emotion filled with fear, with excitement, with tension, with passion, with nerves, with anticipation and above all else with a love so rich it is intoxicating ... a potion I never want to refuse...

Take me in your arms, and hold me there for an eternity...and please do not let me go....you are the core of my existence, and nothing will shake this firm foundation we share, we hold.... If I have not expressed this enough, I do love you Wesley, my love, and am dedicating my life to this wondrous man I now call my husband....a beautiful soul indeed.

LOVE TRAP, SMAT CRAP...

What magic transpires from the controlling of the puppet-*meister*...

When a smooth talking stranger convinces you to part with everything you have...

What sucked me in?
What pulled me tight?
What trapped my mind, believing that this was right...
An escape, my way out...how delicious it tasted,
How susceptible was my spirit to the conundrum awaiting...

How do I explain the toxic effect of this relationship?

The lure, how tempting, I was easy prey. How lucky for the hunter...this one won't go away...Stunned like a deer in the headlights bright, my life stood frozen stiff, panicked in total fright. Far beyond my reality, and dangerously so, compelled to meet expectations, I subjugated fully to threats as meted so. How I fell victim to the pressures of his commands, only to please him, my master, they would be set, and off and onward bound.

In my intoxicated state, drunk on the love notes, the promise of escape, I would function like a wind-up doll and operate. At his whim, do what he said unwittingly, without a second's questioning. The chemical reactions stirring within, had altered my ego, and my id. I was acting way beyond my character, and in my altered state, a stage to perform this drama did begin.

How I reveled in this fantasy...I was engaging in an operation, involved with my lover of sorts, partners in crime, what thrill it gave me this interplay. The drive to meet expectations, of dire circumstance no less, that was the achievement, and how I wanted to prove it...that I was capable, a worthy candidate. I was on a mission, and how fascinating it all seemed, to be part of this quest, ah the intrigue…

The demands were all made via the *messenger* early, at sunrise, amounts already determined. And like the wind-up doll expressed, on switched the buttons, the functions of the day computed and set. With little sleep from the night before, my mind was entangled in the rapture of the dulcet tones of love, of sweet nothingness only to lighten the blow.

I would awaken next morning to the alarm on my phone reminding me the daylight had come, was I ready to go? Appearing alert, but physically and mentally paying the brunt of this curse, I would set off as usual with my mission firm.

Zombie-like in my mental state, on auto-pilot and charged for the day, the next drop, no room for delay. My head brainwashed into believing this was what was expected of me, my duty of great responsibility. My role understood, my focus clear, my mission outlined and ordered. Strapped with the necessary paraphernalia proving legality of my activities, I would with sure footing head to the station. These addresses I had never ventured, thanks to *Google* the ease made it better.

All the while, we would be connected, he, my master, guiding and protecting. Trusting the exchange would take place, he was keen to see the drops completed early within his time frame. I would head to the bank's ATM as soon as the cash dispensers were open, hurry into the corner to withdraw for my services. The limit was sufficient for that day's operation…and off I would go to hunt down the next location.

The frequency of visits, the secession of drops, of demands to be met, raised eyebrows among the local folk. Where was she going they started to ask, among their circles, under the watchful eye. Venturing down more obscure alleyways were these drops to be made. Never before had I been actively involved in the finance of banking; of a frequent resort this was not.

Identification all intact, I would walk in confidently and announce my request. Nerves of steel braced my verve, I was doing this for him, my love, my beau. And with aplomb I would state quite plainly, this was for Egypt, for India, for Africa and for China surely. Here were the details, my next-of kin, my brothers and sisters, what a global union.

They did catch on, these officers here. They sensed the irregularity of my misdeeds. The visitations were too frequent, too closely scheduled, why was she sending so much, all at one time? They started to query further, impending my transaction. The mounting frustration was obvious in my manner; flustered, and fuming, the madam is waiting, I am a *businesswoman*, don't keep me hanging. The computer data was all aflame, bright red across the page. The systems could detect anomalies existing, you were sending this amount where? What was the purpose of this remittance?

Towards the end of this cycle of duties fulfilled, the aversion to such establishments, of my visitations crept on both parties' faces…. The loathing to enter, to handle such requests; the awkwardness of this façade painfully avoiding address… What was she doing with all that money to drop? Had she lost her mind, didn't she realize this was all a hoax?

Closeted from the outside world for far too long, I was not aware of the harsh realities lurking the corridors. News received here was of domestic focus, the rise of the yen, the price of fish at the market. On occasion something of import would be aired, a main event, like the Olympics or World Cup.

A symptom of this country naivety is endemic; of being overly pampered and protected, can be a precarious position to be in. Sadly ill-informed, ignorant to trouble…ah the devilish antics that await beyond the borders. To be aware is to search independently, otherwise The Bastion of Standards and Compliancy would not hear of it.

And there lies the crux of the issue, I had never heard of *romance scams*, never knew they existed. Though plenty abounds in the local language and beyond, of finding a partner, of capturing a heart-throb. Had never entertained the thought of seeking a partner online, was never curious about such services, who would be interested in the profile of mine!

Awoken to the world so severe,

Was I willing to be intrepid,

And journey through this canyon?

But I did.

For the dangers, they were beyond my perception, well past my imagination.

Scams I understood in the conventional sense, but had never scratched its surface, never sniffed its menacing stench… Seeking a niche in society meant cheating your way, ripping people off, taking advantage of their innocence, are we all victims to this game…?

Fooling the unaware, Coercing their minds, Corrupting their affairs… robbing their dignity, Of not playing fair.

Am I supposed to now believe all are knaves, of fraudulent leanings, craving their next opportunity? I cannot blame anyone but myself…

Are you going to punish me for being so gullible...my mind weakened, I was in trouble. Don't look down on me and feel pity...I have gone beyond such superficiality. Wading my way through all of this, I sometimes stop and wince, how was I so stupid from the beginning?

A desperate need for love unrequited, I jumped quickly in that hoop to find a trap well set up, oh my god, how was I duped!

Was I to please my hunter...was I satisfying enough as the hunted?

The bounty at the end was oh so enticing, it was my ticket to escape, my exit from this hostile environment I had grown tired of, had learnt to loathe, even hate. Very little was to sustain me here other than a few contacts, dear students, who, on occasion had made me feel, for a brief moment, normal, real, had extended kindness generously enough to enable a firmer footing here.

Self-loathing had crept in, depression had lurked its ugly head, my dignity all shattered like fine-bone china on the concrete slab.

Naturally I was led to think my 'pop-up' to be the solution, the answer to my issues...and I responded. How corrupted of spirit had I become.

In this transition now visible before me, the prevailing remained obscure; hidden to those dear in my circle. I was distant and distracted, bound by this other world; of operations, of master threats, who would have known what spheres I was possessed.

Occasionally the phone would ring. In a gravelly voice he would begin:
'You are the one, you are mine,
What are you talking about?
With God's blessing, we will unite.'
You may ask what the purpose of *all that money was*,
To save a sinking ship, secure loot, gold pieces. Both literally... no really!
In hindsight it all sounds a bit hyperbolical, in what day and age are we confronted with such diabolical???

A sense of danger approaching the rough seas, a darkening of skies, a foreboding mirage looming?
Where's the money, how much can you drop?
Please believe me my dear this has to stop.
One more deposit, one more exchange,
One more arrow, one more cage.
The façade we uphold, maintaining a story,
Keeping faith on hold...why do we do what we do?

I could easily block the *app* and withdraw from view.

Why don't you screams my head? I can't... persists my heart...there is so much unfinished business yet, why do I tread?

I have given him my all, what am I dreaming...a win fall?

I doubt very positively that this will eventuate, with bated breath, I have more than anticipated the outcome of my fate.

Just one more drop, one more deal. How do you think I feel?

I am not your money-bags dear, I don't even earn that much. Do you now want me to turn tricks for you, my love, so as to keep this end of the deal? An affront...

I struggle to find solutions yet cannot resist the constant interruption that exists.

Hold me strong and don't let go....

Dear God intervene... I am not of substance, and my nerves are wearing thin....

I indulge him, to keep the channels alight, but at what cost to this blight?

Am I letting go or standing still, is there any promise to fulfill? I doubt it.

My circumstances have proven thus far, there is nothing to gain from this affair.

I have not had a pleasant ride, it has not taken me afar, no delight transpired.

Stunted I look for answers and to my dismay, there is nothing but a vacant stare, dull and lifeless, but a pallor veneer reflected in vain.

How do I overcome this dilemma?

Give up immediately and flee forever? What options are presented, what to hold, life is not perfect, accept and move on?

Frustratingly, and in vain, I seek an angle, sometimes bemusing my innermost emotions...Temporarily relieving my thoughts racing in my mind, I then return to the same vicious cycle, weathered over time. Must I surrender to these impasses, or do I valiantly proceed without disaster? The prospects foreboding, the will disturbed, my mind ever confused...pray be still.

There a sumo *yukata*-clad, balancing precariously on his bicycle, he rides past by me oblivious to the stares. In what world am I surrounded, confusion only blares.

A curiosity for certain, inquisitive glances only remind me of the differences existing. I sit in wonder, where will this lead me, am I going to carry such a burden for too much longer? Will he concede and reprieve on the offer?

Letter 16:

You have ignited in me a fire so strong, burning inside of me, that not even an ocean of water can put out...this longing for you permeates my body and my mind.... The magnetic force drawing me closer to you ...I can no longer resist....I surrender!

The current of passion within me touches my core so deeply ....I am dizzy with emotion....is the earth below me moving or am I spinning out of control?...how the force of one man, my husband sway me in such a way...there are no answers...

Yet chemistry is what scientists suggest...the compatibility of each other based on the blending of character....our exchange goes beyond chemistry....this wondrous mystery undefinable......

I know you are with me now... you have taught me how to perceive this sensation, to recognize your presence, and welcome the intense glow of your being.... as a celestial being from above, a rare but precious sighting can only be conceived when truly connected....and that is us....a bonding so complete, a circle so perfect....a love so pure...

How could I have ended here....blessed with the greatest gift of all... you have offered me a most valuable possession...the recognition of love... in all its dimensions, its depths, its widths and more....you have taught me to cherish each moment as if it were your last...to hold life in both hands, and never take anything for granted, you have convinced me that life is a wondrous journey, the beauty of nature supreme.

How much have you done for me....beyond comprehension...you have unlatched my soul, have given me freedom to express myself no matter how clumsy it seems, and to revel in this beauty of love you constantly offer....I have reached a stage farther than the peaks, way beyond the clouds...am with you in a state of heavenly bliss all because of you, my husband and king...the dearest and sweetest man I have ever known... my love Wesley

Do Not Forsake Me, Oh My Darling,

Courageous, might we venture forth,
Your presence what joy there is to hold,
Unbridled, your love being our light…
Yet cajoled and confounded midway,
What burden is this, distrust at play?
And what if I swoop down low,
Pity on me, if I crash and fall?
Wanting so much for this to be, yet cannot force nature upon thee.
Hope for the day we unite, yet quietly doubt the fulfillment and delight.
What becomes the soul, wretched and blighted,
A shadow of gloom on the horizon takes might.
A force that chokes this, my reality tight,
I *beg* you uphold the end of the bargain, to see the light....

So what happens when confronted with life's great hurdles? Are we bound to blunder, flounder and fall?

When at the tipping point our reactions become irrational, our perspective warped and twisted, the filter be coated with rose-colored tint. The cliches abound, yet when in the midst of heated arousal, passions flood the mind incomprehensible. How, one wonders, can it be any other, convinced the words expressed are from the one; my lover.

Struggling to counter measure, this shift of balance, the oscillation; forces rational persist, listen to your head, yet the heart beats insist.

Lovesick, an oxymoron of intrigue; being sick and in love, being sick with love, being sick of love, an equilibrium of sorts complete. What nonsense is spouted, what illogic is this? Yet all the while courting the very factor malignant, yearning for the great white knight to serve, protect and shelter ...from the oppressive circumstances at my table.

How dare you prick this cushion of comfort, shielding me from your corruption. Struggling as I do on a daily basis to make head and tail of this madness. Of mind, I am not stable, but soar at great heights far beyond the skies in flight. How magical this vision beams, yet the niggling persists, what if...? This reality transposed remains a fragment of my imagination, a fantasy made up as a coping mechanism to my plight manacled, and fettered.

I sit and observe in wonder the machinations at play, the inconsistencies of behavior, anomalies unrestrained.

How dare you come closer and afflict pain!

No more!

My resistance, my defenses, my guard on high you can no longer penetrate this space I occupy. All pervasive, I won't let you in, charged though you may appear, ignorant yes, how dare you impose your agenda within.

A self- fulfilled prophecy I do admit, this course has been long, yet the endurance resists. Wreaking despotism, this world survives, beyond thy boarders, above the skies. Remain all closeted my dear friends, for the truth will ring loudly in judgment.

How fervent my convictions stand...never have they weakened, nor stumbled headlong into the abyss of sham (e.) Languishing in your cultural strain has done nothing to ease the pain. Refracted and mislabeled, the vision I clearly see, a people who are desperate to be free, of the clutches of societal constraints, the notion of liberation only a faint refrain.

What shakes the bedrock of my foundations, a fertile mind filled with escape in imagination?

Don't play havoc with my head son! Only the test of time will prove you wrong. Blemishes on the surface, they will not stain, but licked and healed, they are but a smear, a smudge impermanent.

Stay focused and at peace with all, they are not at fault that their system is flawed. Be humble and grateful despite the attacks on my survival. Confusion remains, yet perseverance ticks eternal.

Treading the mill of life with ease
My mind lost in the clouds afloat
What pleasure this gives.
Though my heart still restless,
Calm seeping in this glow.
Why would I want any other?
The pestering, the dissonance,
How I have longed for comfort.
Be assured he will meet his Maker,
All aflame on a great pyre.
Bless those who must endure,
Pain withering over time,
But a dull murmur vapid…
Cosmetic and scar-free, I am me.

Letter 17:

How I deserve to be with a guy as beautiful as you!

Clearly you are dedicated to honoring your word, kind and considerate at all times, a character so noble you stand a giant among men...and you are prepared to come to my doorstep...how do I deserve this?

Braving the high seas, the potential dangers awaiting the waters, sailing half way around the world primarily for work but also to see me here...in a land way off your regular route, I am beside myself...who takes such action? Someone very special, highly committed, or completely crazy?

Such grand gestures invoke in me a sense of amazement, wondrous at the fact that you would make such a plan for me....what can I say.... here I am.....I am yours...

This world I have been privy to, your world, is one exciting and highly charged...I am attracted to the spontaneity, the urgency, the danger, and the surprise....but mostly to the outpouring of your soul, the sensitivity and honesty and more importantly the love you express....this cannot be denied...

Through our special moments we have shared, you have allowed me insight into your mind, how you feel, what you think...and frankly despite the oceans or distance that divides we have become one and the same reflection...your emotion, your passion, raise the bar of attraction... and how I love you so.....

I cannot doubt you Wesley...you have proven time and time again that you are real, this is real, what we are doing is real, and a new reality does really await us in the not so distant future...What has happened in the brief passage of time only proves the power of your love, the impact you have made on me, the commitment to your word....

GALAXY

The Galaxy that exists; let me explain this so called reality
    One where the mind is constantly questioning its 24 -carat reliability.
    There are the Sundays when a congregation meets,
    They go to the **church** but I think it is a euphemism for something else…
    A cult, a clan, a brotherhood, a cohort, a gang of sorts,
    And where was it again, you say Bahrain or lying off the west coast,
    Somewhere in the sea in proximity to the continent?
    The network works wonders at sniffing you out,
    Discovered on Google the coordinates of your current hide-out.
    How lucky for you to be sailing the seven seas,
    With my pretty penny in the pocket, a globetrotting life of ease.
    Makes me curdle inside and brings me dis-ease.
    The mind creates this framework to compensate for the irrational, the illogical. For six months on, the conditions remain, whereby a ransom be paid, another drop of sheer urgency, to secure the loot, of *filthy* lucre hidden away… that will someday be here, you say, early in the day. You have got to be joking admits the logical side, it is a trap…yet reminders from dear Sunny Jacob keep intermittently being sent…

Dear customer,
    The termination of your holdings in our storage will take heed.
    Cover the fees promptly or lose it completely.
    Lose what I beg? My savings are all depleted, I have nothing more to lose, take it I surrender.
    This world, where interplanetary connections network indiscriminately, preys on the frailty of systems. Like viral spores, *they* keep savagely weakening

the immunity, a blanket of security infested. Not protected? Pull the plug and disconnect, no other option to escape.

Where are the law-enforcements I hear you say? The notion of privacy, an ideal once cherished, now leaves us fully defenseless in our vulnerability. The whims of malevolence infiltrating with their presence, they being the Big Brother's adversary, the Black Knight of hackers, the strategists with a mission, to plunder and pillage, that of a by- gone tradition.

With modern tools at hand, they stealthily encroach, the system we entrust only loosely securing the surface. The infrastructure at play, is weak and leaking, a system so sick, the unravelling such a blessing for the hoodwinkers persisting. Their clandestine operations, no detection is made of their malicious operations…beyond the system, beyond the law, a paradigm shift feeding into their own coffers, unleash the RATs, let the invasion begin!

There exists submerged in the deepest, darkest chasm, a whole other world, a parallel universe if you will, interconnected. Acting in ways more pernicious, simply put vicious. To the naked eye, we cannot perceive the vandalism of the viral cataclysm undertow. With every breathing moment the web ticks over, exhorting their conniving ways yet to be surfaced.

How is one defended from the dragons breathing down your throat? Switch it off and ignore it? Was once, an option for the cold callers of a bygone era. They reside in your system, flooding and clogging the veins of your communication; that which defines your very existence.

The penetration immeasurable afflicting the networked system, once thought of as a selling tool for your convenience. Raiding sources, stealing details and data…how foolish we have become in relying on such a complex matrix of integers.

And what of the corrupting channels? Who do you turn to when forcibly violated? There is no hard evidence, no weapon, no scars, nothing visibly detected. Faith in the order sullied by man's duplicity…how does one overcome and survive unscathed anonymity?

Given the fast-paced ever-changing progress marked in *IT*, laws cannot even decipher the principles of restriction nor define their application.

Let chaos take over, let the cracking thwart existence,

Until another fall victim?

How long do we wait, how much do we endure,

At what point do we stop and give attention to the menacing threat,
Playing havoc in the system, and with my head?

Where is the succour when sorely needed? Ah the cavalier pretense. Not of particular interest? Not of concern? We have more important issues to undergo.

Have some data, some information of interest…do you *not* want to at least take a look at the issue?

My sources?

The very weakness of system, the faulty connections, not hermetically sealed for your protection.

Such a leak, such a link, have mercy on me!

Curiosity screams, the pursuit of investigation weighs high, a glimpse into their world inadvertently transpires. A fraternity of members, from all corners of the globe, non- gender specific, how coming- of-age the posse has become. Off the shores in the Atlantic or Pacific or both, a vessel afloat and fully equipped, where a gang of profiteers subsists.

Who are you? Where do you come from? This cartel of thieves, a consortium of diversity as evidenced in the listing of languages: of English, Arabic, Vietnamese and Thai, a sprinkling of European strains strategically selected to add fuel to the marauding on nigh. Working in tandem on an assignment, you sense there are a few engaged on any one project: *en masse* this violation, of scamming and cheating the innocent.

Have you paid off enough for your presence afloat in the bay …oh what a haven. Of disparate individuals forging a fraternity; the collusion of criminality, I just *pray* that guilt does afflict your barometer of morality. Sadly though temptation has corrupted the soul, and sucked you dry, stung you permanently…scarred you for dear life…the long lost sons and daughters… Wickedly divisive, yours is one of rage; a fire burning in desperation, you know no other.

Stepping outside the system, what a dare! By sheer connection, my eyes wide open to the very function of manipulation, with not a gram of pity spared. Incorrigible in pursuits, you flagrantly rape the minds of your young female victims.

What is worst you toyed with her spirit, played with her mind, destroyed her confidence and scarred her outlook on life. Yet beyond all of this, she has wizened to your ways, she has learnt to overcome such terror, and is more determined these days.

Where do you sit so mighty and high,
Another Galaxy, another planet, beyond the sky?
How does it look from your angle there,
By my own admonition, a reproachable character.
Can you see me as you sit and stare?
Ah the cohort of thieves,
Attempting to wrest her precious dignity,
Do you know just how this feels?
Confounded I am left lamenting the depravity of character,
And beg for mercy, a slither of compassion.

Letter 18:

Love does really exist and what you have done is drawn it out of me....you have touched a nerve so sensitively, realized the essence of my nature, and motivated me to strive for it in a way I have never known....what you have done is nurtured my soul, feed me a diet of love and respect, and stimulated my eagerness to follow you ...even to the ends of this world, and the next...

To be with you and stand side by side with you makes me feel so happy... thoughts running through my head, of what you said or did, constantly puts a smile on my face...I could be waiting for a train, then suddenly a memory of you flashes across my mind...I am now in a blissful state...those recent photos of you are so dear...have been staring at them all day...they keep reminding me of the wonderful man I have grown attracted to, the guy I call my husband...who wouldn't be happier with a beautiful soul...I love you my dear Wesley.

WHEREFORE ART THY ROMEO?

Where does this leave us, my charming one. I despair to think, this will end quickly, all will be done. You have entered my space, my head, my heart; just shutdown, abandon and stop?

Lift me out of this troubled state, give me the confidence to embrace a vision of fate, please give me faith. With all the signs pointing positively, the stars in my horoscope, they are aligned, indicating improvement they have told me.

Yet the cavernous cell remains, empty, hollow and forsaken. Failing to mend this punctured state, has left me deflated, not so poised as before.

When will this end?

Although disconnecting, fast approaching complete dissociation, the lines are left alive for communication.

The saccharine I have overly indulged, has left me wired and shaky, frankly never had a sweet tooth since I was a child.

Your notes leave me de-sensitized beyond caring.

I do not feel,

I do not think,

I do not need your pity,

I will persist despite the adversity.

To survive is to buffer any sentimentality.

Maudlin indulgence only fuels the negativity.

How disempowered I *could* feel, yet I will not surrender for public appeal.

In this world, and with the right channels, justice will be served.

I must have faith in the system, to behold.

Where do I go from here? I wonder. 'The world is your oyster,' I continually hear blasted. How fortunate for me, to have my health, my head still committed to serve and uphold. Yet quietly my heart is flooded with tears, pierced so severely, the draining of red, like the Arctic flow currently bleeding. A stopgap for the damage, what do I do, drop everything and run for the hills?

Comfort Station

You may ask where I jot down such words, such messages, such prose.

I shut myself away from all the noise and find shelter in what I like to coin *the office*, where I sit on my throne. In common parlance it is no other than the wash room, the toilet or *il gabinetto;* my comfort station.

For me, it is the quietest spot away from all the prattle, the conspiring, and gibberish found in the local hangouts. In a word my inner sanctum, affording me peace of mind from the chaos encroaching.

A throne like no other!

With all the bells and whistles, yes, the Japanese will go to such extent to promote the ease of relief without feeling quite so self -conscious.

Have you had the *washlet* experience?

Fascination with the lower regions, and how to facilitate deliverance let's say, we find hoses adjusted at all angles, fans and sprays, serving what appears an endless number of functions for the duties demanded. Mounted on the wall you can find the touch panel screen, selecting the position and intensity according to need; bespoke at its supreme!

It can be a little daunting at first.

Jets of water from high pressured hoses are ready to shoot up between you…best to close the legs a little. The sprays are not only designed for pleasure, they get in there, every nook and cranny, every crease checked assuming the surface bacterium is eliminated. You can play all day long but I have business to attend, not of the nether regions mind you ….not!

In between appointments, I have time for myself. I can sit for at least an hour uninterrupted, immersed in my work; tapping away, corresponding to emails, the 'lover's' messages and what not. It is where arrangements are made, confirmations of details set, contracts to be claimed. I could happily remain here resting atop, inconspicuous, hidden away from *that lot*.

Occasionally the guard comes in to inspect. Invariably a man, with a perfunctory manner; just performing 'my duty' kind of fashion. He doesn't worry me so much. Provided the cubicle door is locked, and the recorded background water trickle is 'on.' There is someone here, is the warning made.

Now that I have a better grip on things to date, the responses to the 'lover's' requests don't fool me in the same way. I have got used to his brusque demands, but have learnt to play along for interest's sake.

Sadomasochistic in some warped and obtuse way…the physical threat non apparent, affords me the pleasure to be entertained, to feed my curiosity, to understand his nature…so sick and weird some would say. The interaction at play pries open an element in my life very hard to explain. Our conversations as such, though harmless at first, are imbued with the burning desire to perform, to deliver, to produce. The pressure to gratify the exigencies, are at the forefront of any interaction. We continue to tiptoe gently around in circles, until the parameters are bound tightly, choking, there is no escaping from the enclosure.

Time consuming I know, it is the banter I indulge. Willingly I chat, and delight in the sexual innuendo. Besides, he has all my savings, there is nothing more in the takings. For stringing him on, yes, I am foolish to mollify his ways. But I truly pity him, preying on defenseless women, and messing with their minds, tormenting and forcing them to comply.

Ironically it is for the sake of the system here in Japan that has saved my butt!

Admittedly, and for whatever reasons impervious to me, I am no longer able to remit any amounts overseas. Such attempts through the various channels, and I have got to know a few might I say, are branded red, of danger alarming, obvious consternation in my head. Despite the change of addresses, the relocation, the systems have forbidden me any access to *all* the global regions.

Ironically it is for this fact that I am truly grateful. I am my worst enemy when it comes to vicious cycles. I overcome and then have relapses…thank goodness, I haven't turned into a coke -snorting addict, nor a gambler. But the traits are very similar, that is how I function, a bit depressing really, but I have learnt to curb these indulgences. For it is the system that forbids me any further operation. And strangely, perhaps for the first time ever, I am beholden to its conservative regulations.

ADDENDUM

The incidences occurring in this account are true, can be verified, and in some cases are still ongoing today. To date, no assistance has been offered in resolving this dilemma despite endeavors to seek advice from authorities both here in Japan, Australia and The U.S. These issues remain with neither pursuit of investigation, nor protection legal or otherwise.